Her Blood and Bone

To Nisa and Ernie

Flying Dodo Publications
Bellingham, WA
flyingdodopublications.com
angela@flyingdodopublications.com
ISBN 978-0-9970111-4-2
10 9 8 7 6 5 4 3 2 1   18 19 20 21

First printing, 2018

Printed in the United States of America.

Her Blood and Bone

by Angela Boyle

Flying Dodo Publications · Bellingham, Washington

Beatrix has always been one to keep on top of trends. In 1869, Frederick Myers published a patent for a single-wheeled "velociped." In 1881, another unicycle was patented by Battista Scuri. Not wanting to fall behind the times, Beatrix was one of the first to adopt the unicycle as her main mode of transportation. While she has found that she gets places faster, she has also found that she arrives quite disheveled. With the voluminous skirts of the late 1800s, it is not much of a surprise.

European badger, *Meles meles*

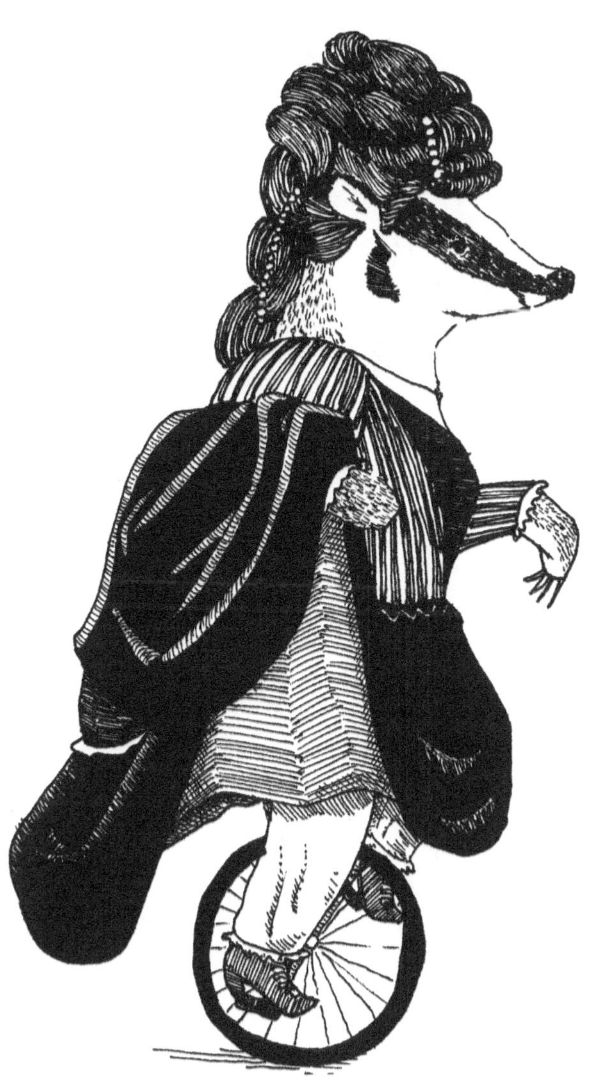

Clarissa and Aryana are complete and utter hams. Ask them to perform or pose, then try to stop them. You will fail. The only thing they enjoy more than performing is clams. So I suppose that is how you would stop them. Offer them clams.

walrus, *Odobenus rosmarus*

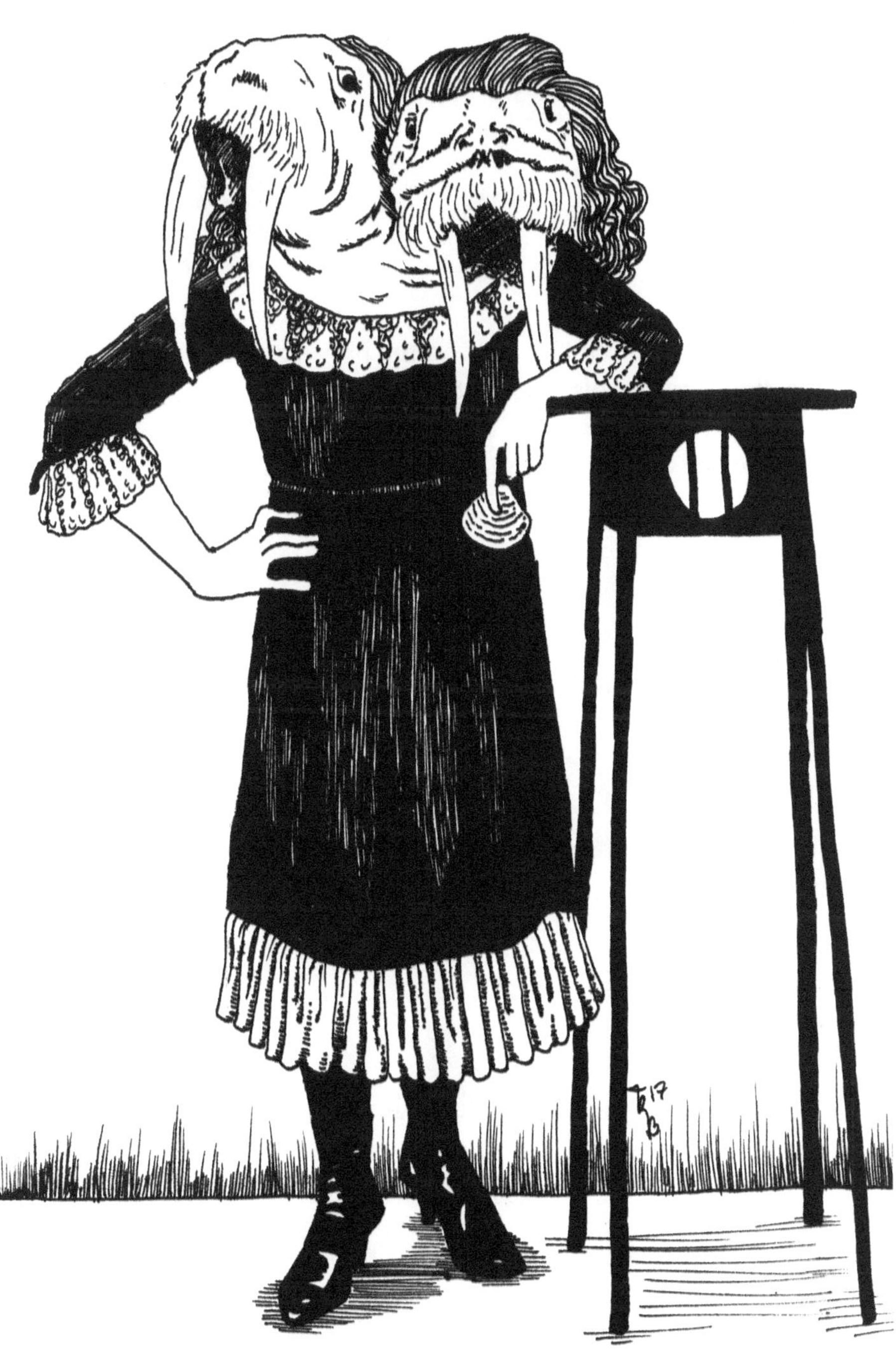

Rosalind is a Victorian lady on the prowl. Hunting in the labor district of the Black Country, she pulls out her blow-gun to shoot down her next victim. Having not yet been caught, we have no idea what she does with these unfortunate souls.

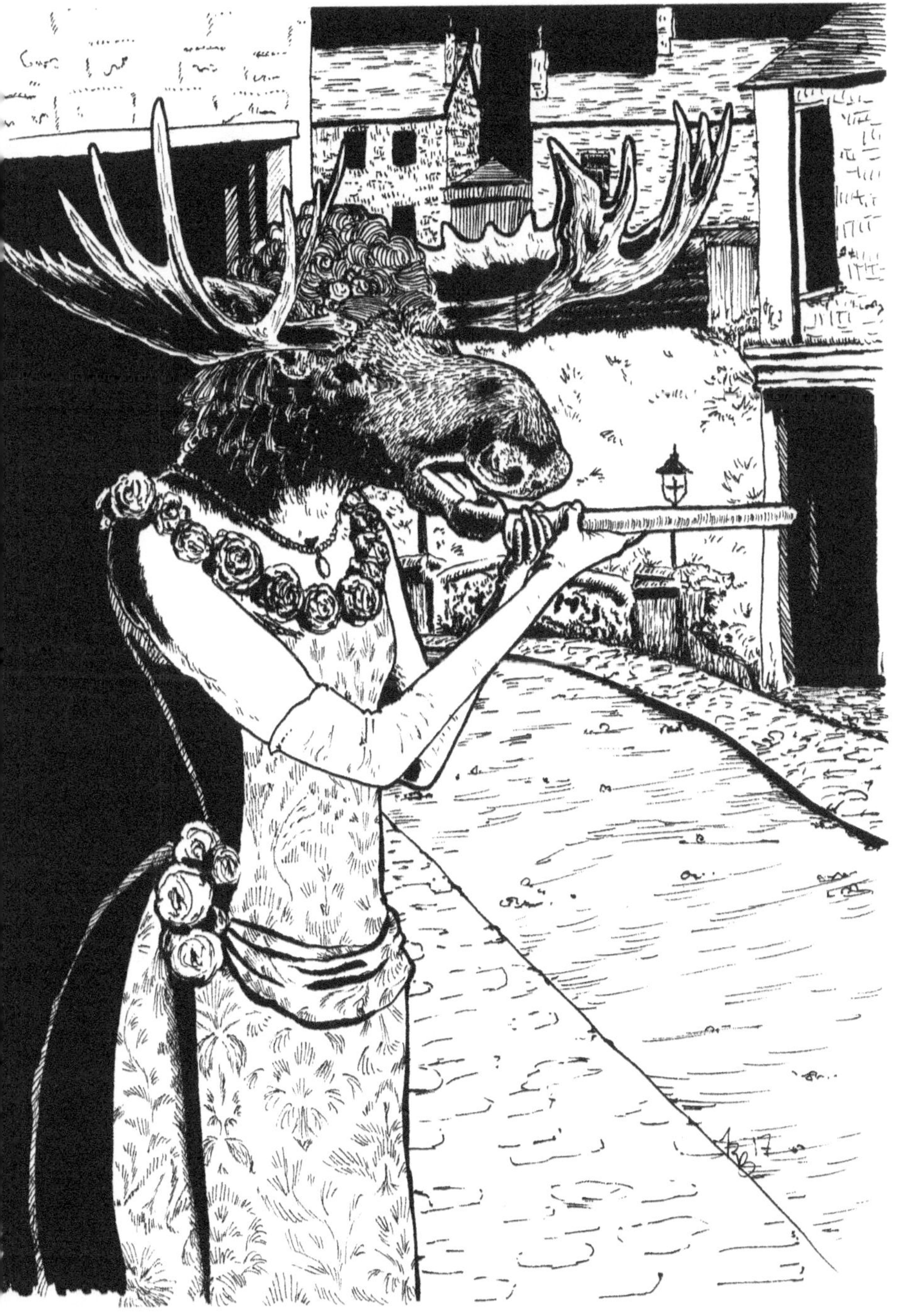

Natalie loves to swim. She owns more swim suits than any other piece of clothing. Almost more than all her other clothes combined. She has left multiple partners, even though they garnered her deep affection, when she found out they don't like to swim. At least she learned her lesson after trying to force her first partner into swimming . . .

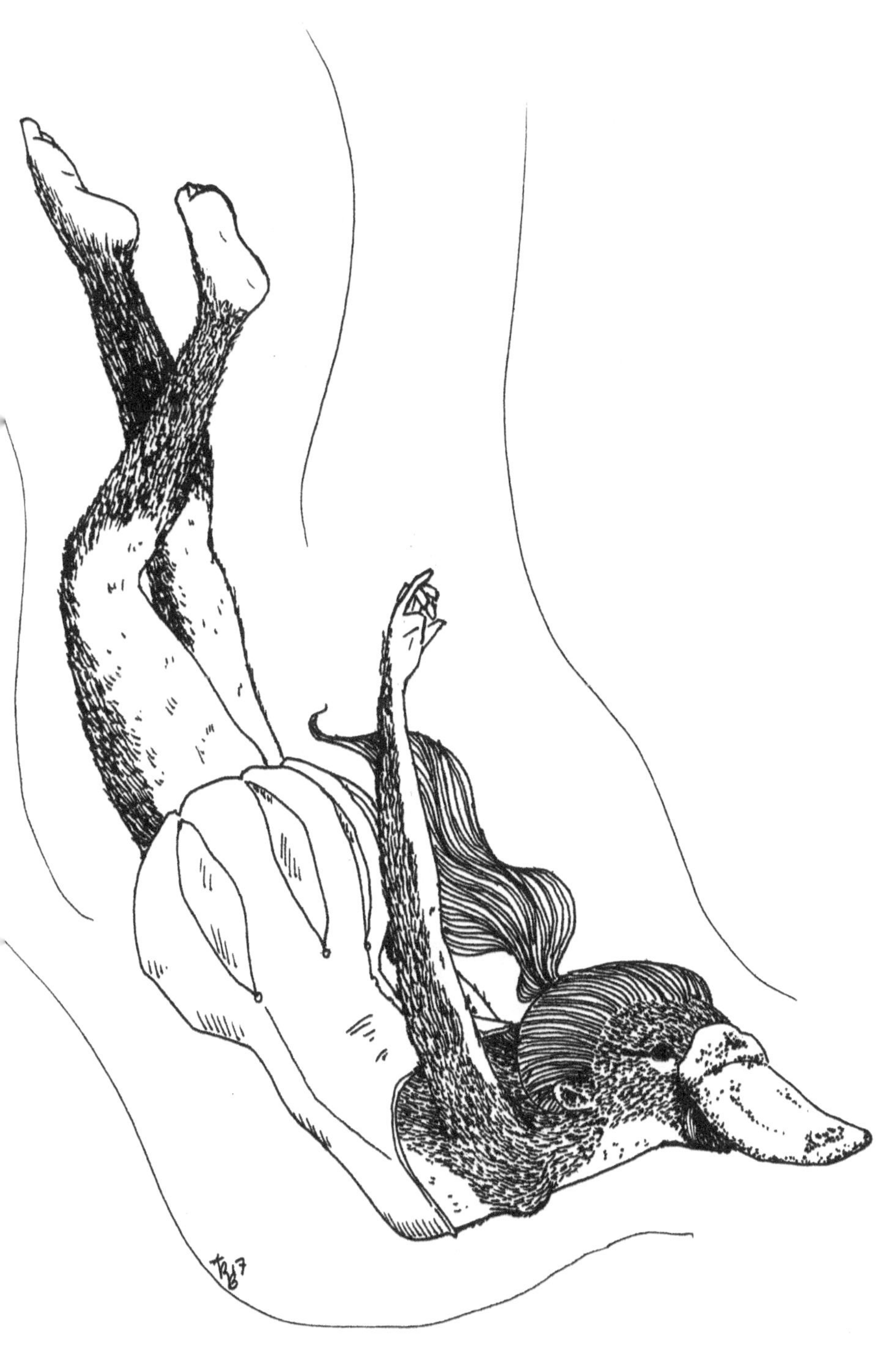

Alejandra just wants to dance. She has been seen dancing at the park and in the subway. At the top of the Empire State Building. Below the Eiffel tower. Along train tracks and at the edge of the Aurora Bridge. She almost danced off the edge of the Grand Canyon, but a nearby tourist caught her.

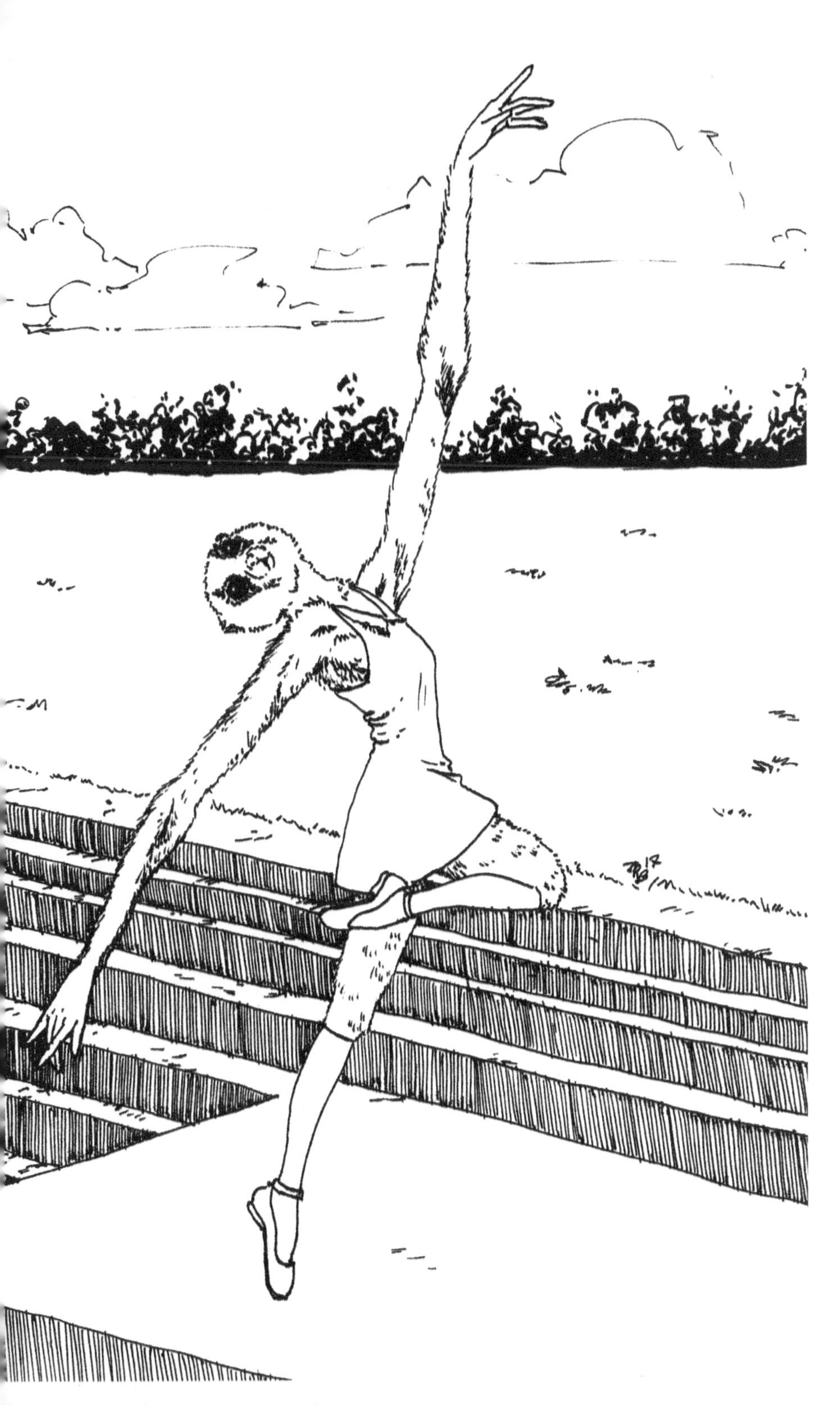

*J*oanna feels the tug of desire both to hunt and to protect. With her sword, she tries to accomplish both, but sometimes her thoughts get muddled and she can't remember who she is saving from what, or why she is hunting someone. So she takes a break on a bridge and thinks. She focuses on the sound of the water and lets it calm her mind.

anglerfish, *Caulophryne pelagica*

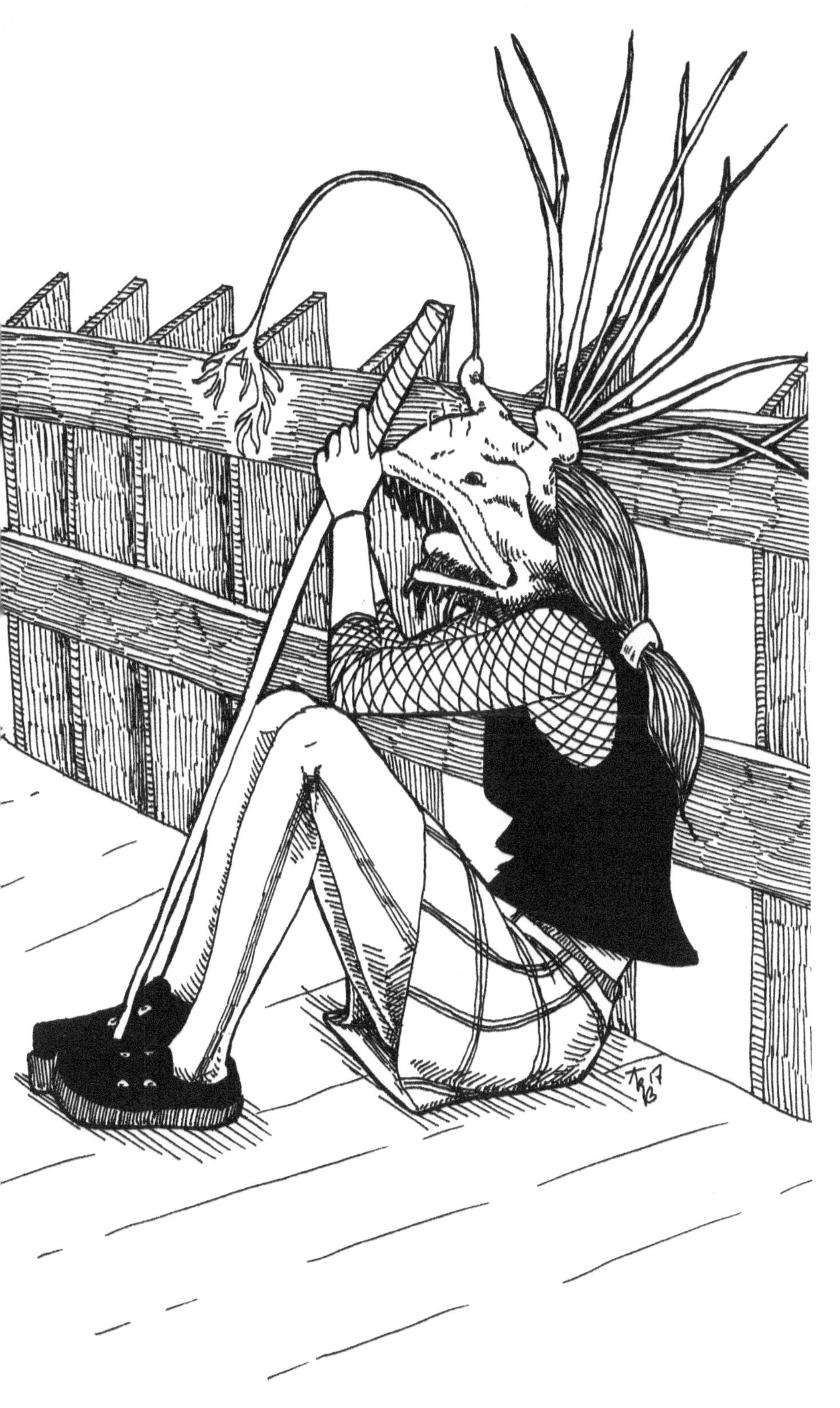

etty is a shy sloth. She carries a kercheif with her everywhere so she can hide when she gets too overwhelmed. But if you do sneak a momentary interaction with her, she is one of the sweetest people you could hope to meet. You would never guess she keeps a collection of blood in antique ink bottles in her basement.

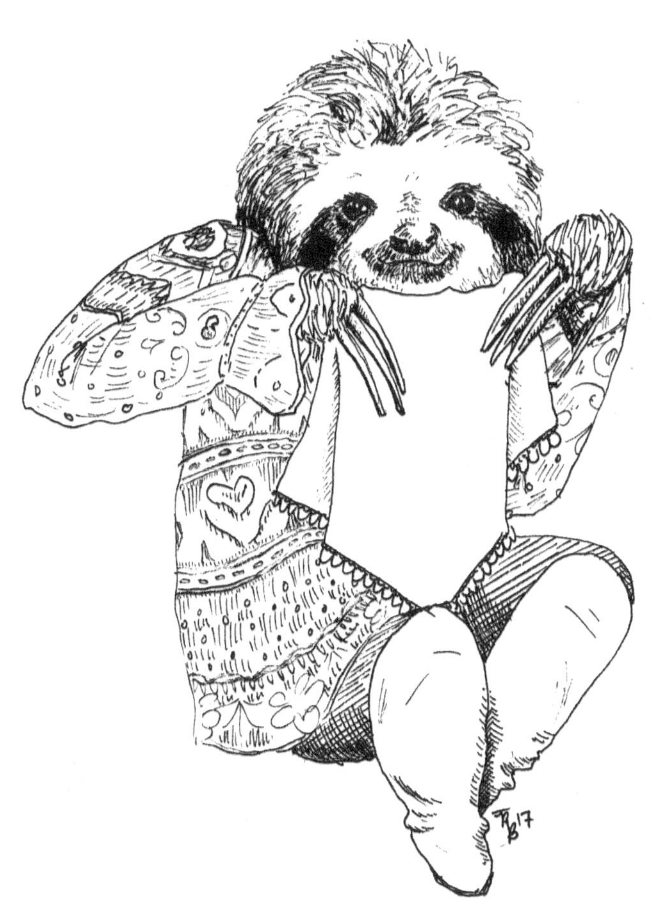

$\mathcal{M}$attie is a young lady who was born with a club foot. After extensive surgeries as a toddler, she was all straightened out. As a tween, she had to wear a back brace to cure her scoliosis. And then as a teen, she also had to get braces to straighten her teeth after getting an extra one removed. Despite her body trying to twist itself into a corkscrew, she is good-natured and always trying to cheer up those around her.

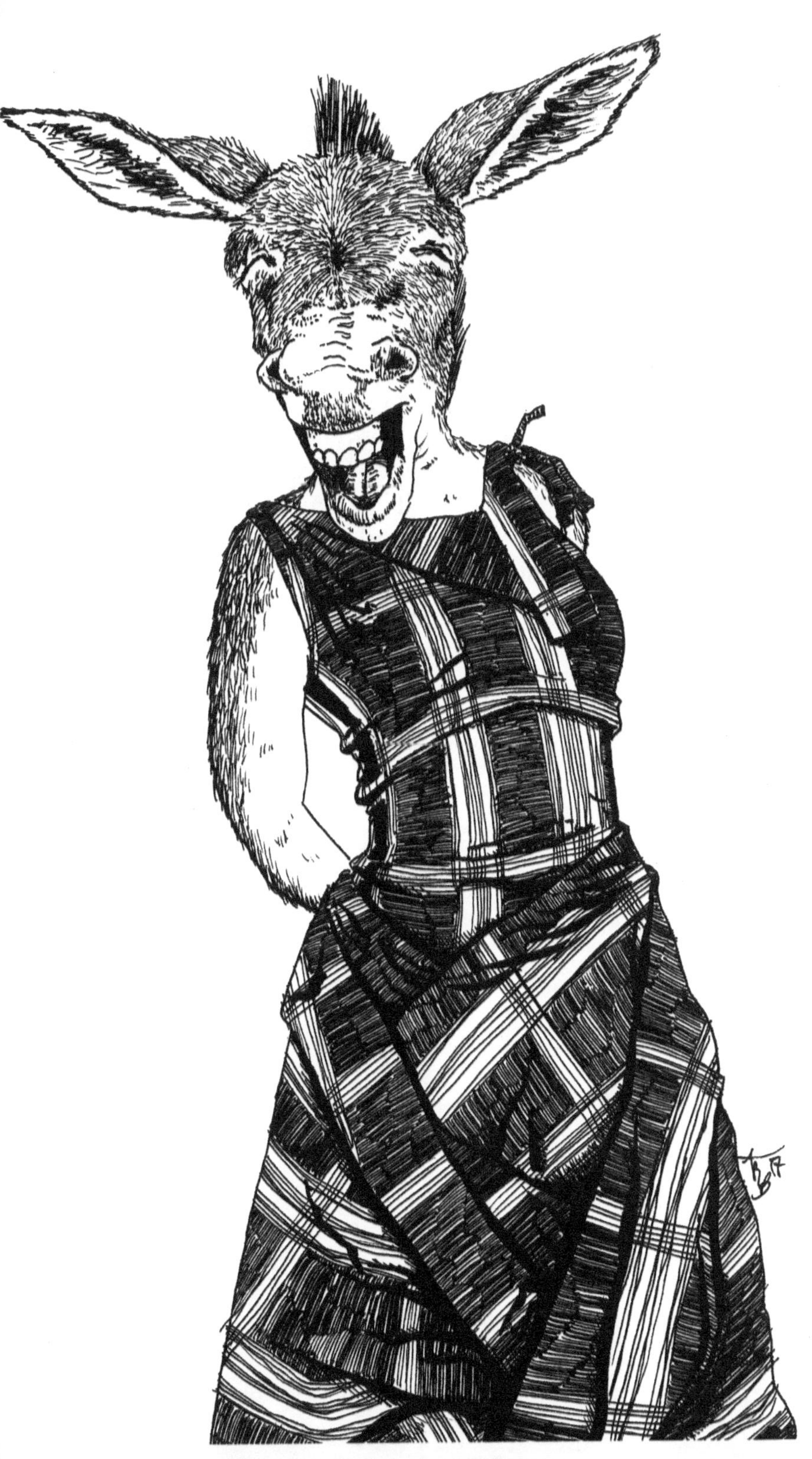

Lucy was kidnapped from New York as a young girl. She was kept by her captor for just over three years in the sewers of Hong Kong before she freed herself by hitting him over the head with a pipe she dug out of the wall with her bare hands. It took her five months to get the pipe out. Now she works at a cat cafe, still in Hong Kong, and returns to the sewer just to scream. And scream. And scream.

Tasmanian devil, *Sarcophilus harrisii*

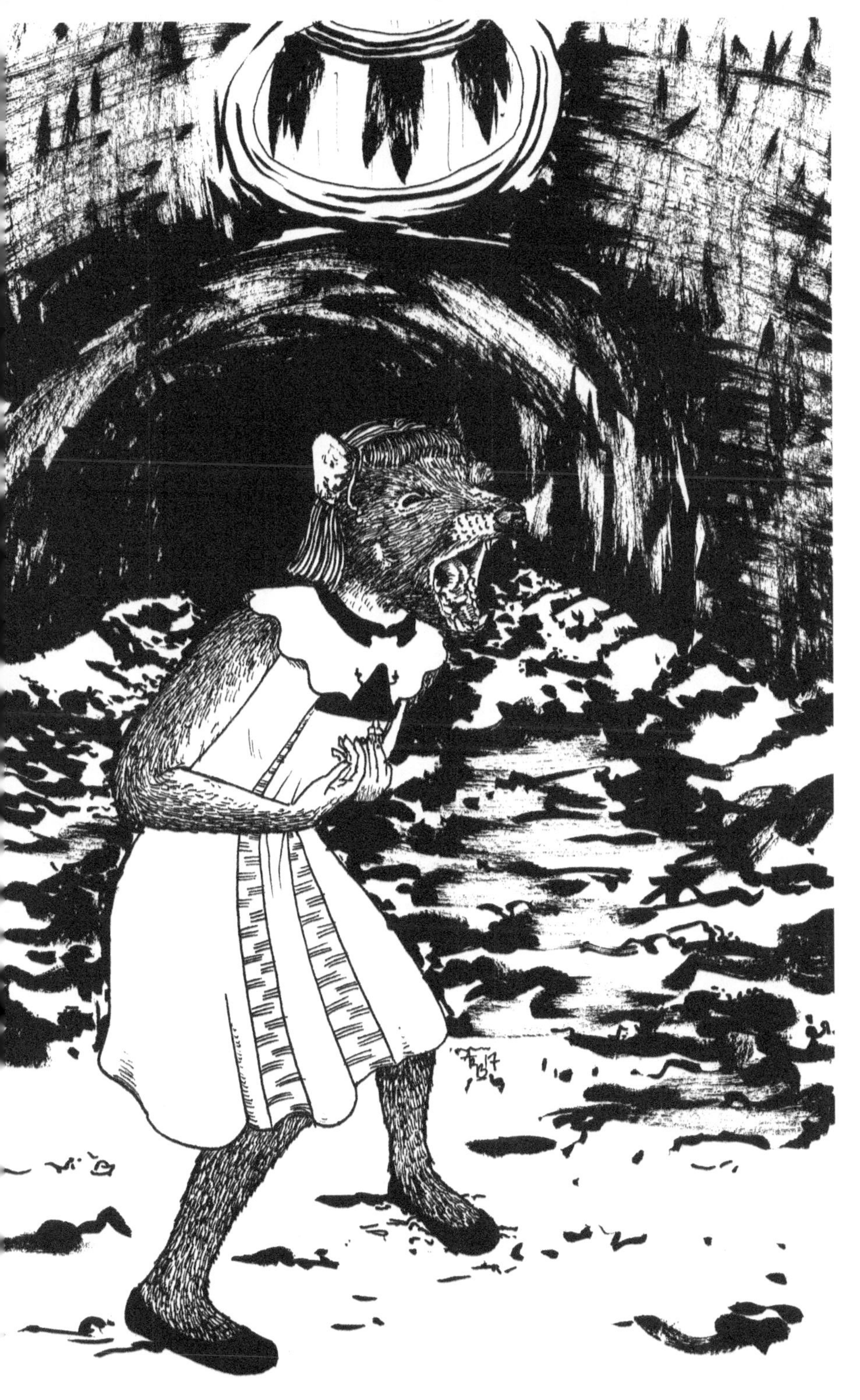

Jocelyn loves to dance. She loves to dance with her tiny cuttlefish friends. Unfortunately, her friends are much smaller than she is and sometimes she gets too exuberant. It's a good thing cuttlefish are a dime a dozen.

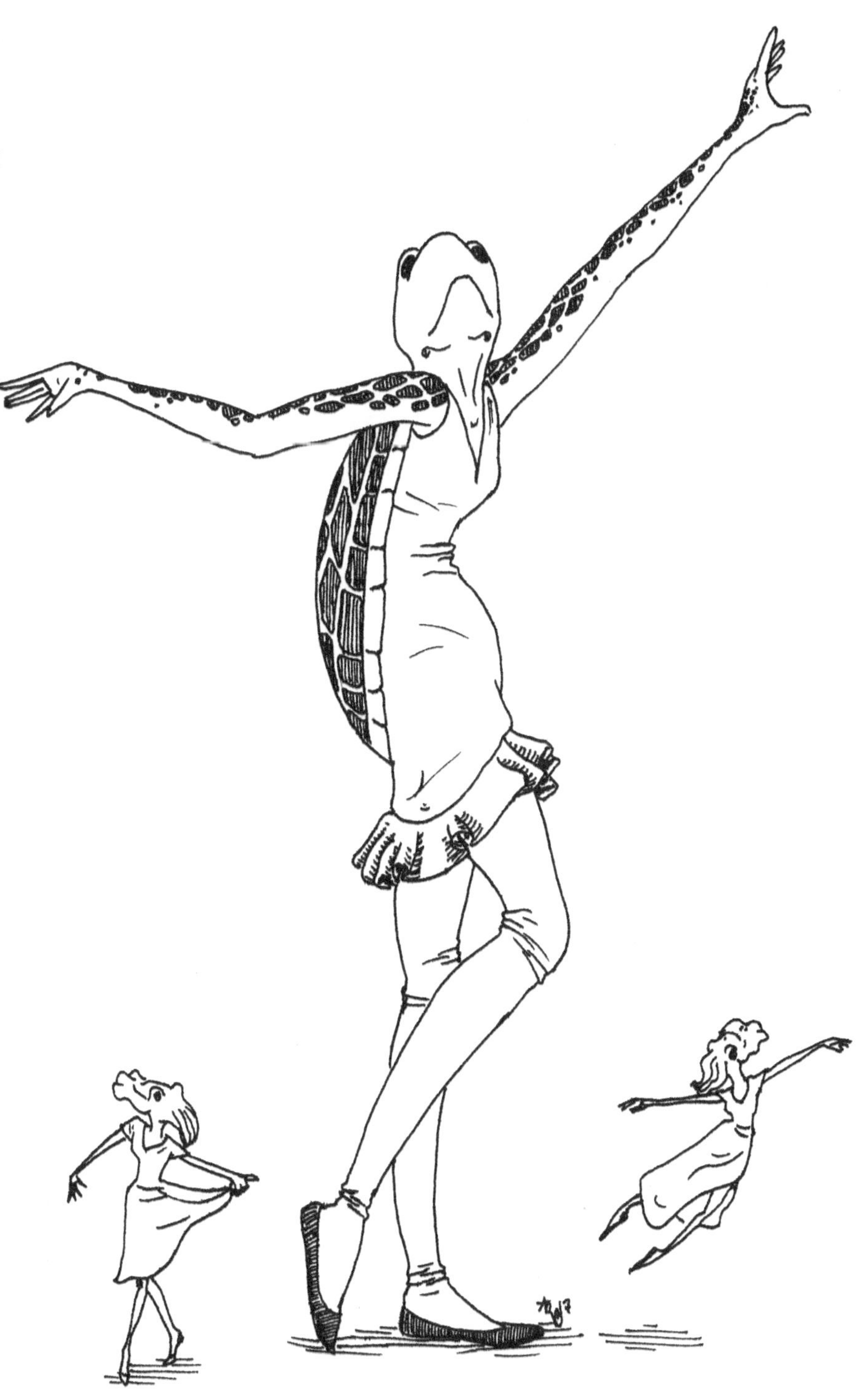

lianna is a young lady who has never learned to drive. Unfortunately for her, she also never learned to leave on time and is always running for the bus. She once leapt in front of a bus that she was trying to catch as it started to pull away. Fortunately, the driver was paying attention for once.

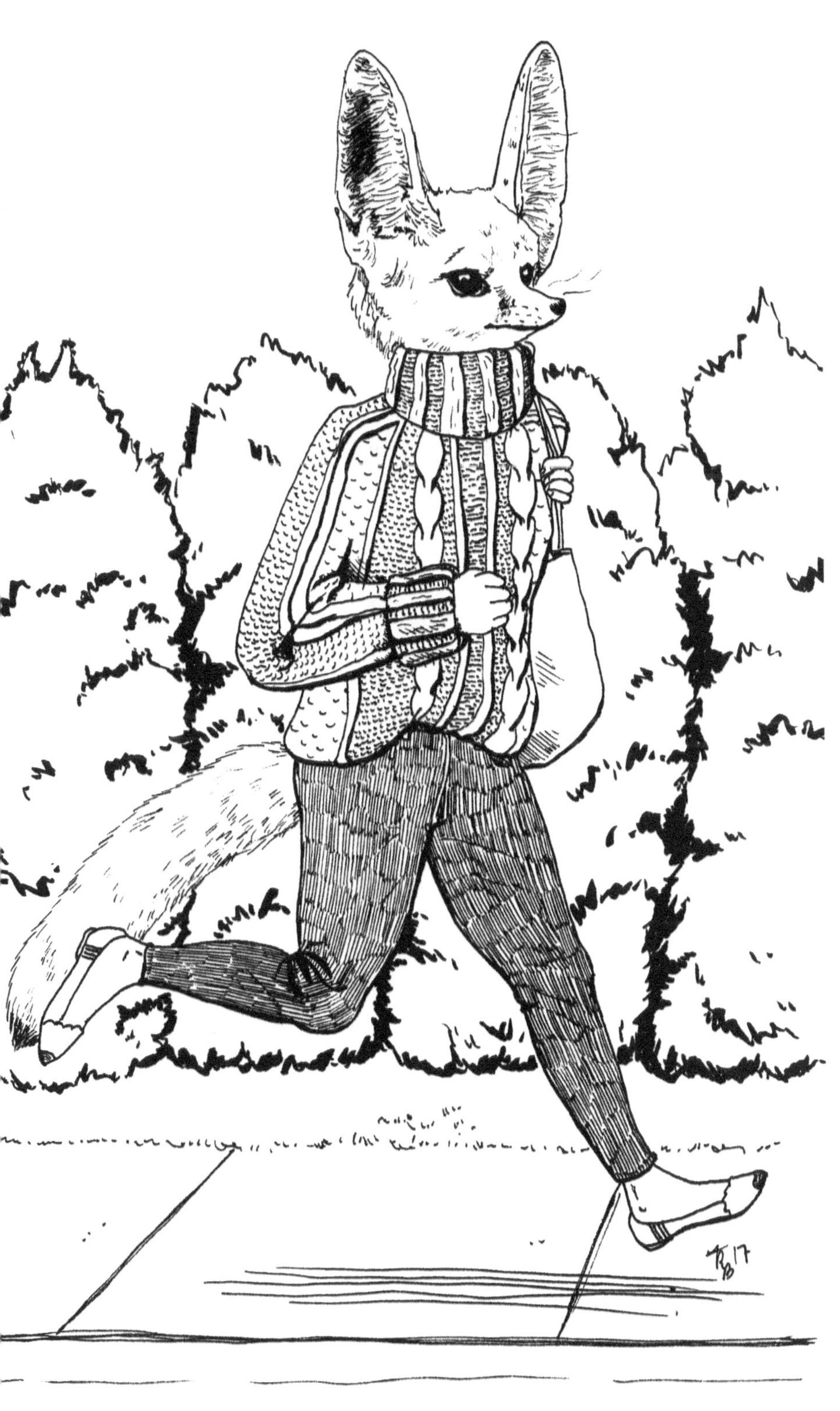

Laney has a bulging disc. It comes and goes. Sometimes the pain shoots down her legs and they give way. Lifting is an important part of her job. She needs to start remembering to lift the bodies with her knees, not her back.

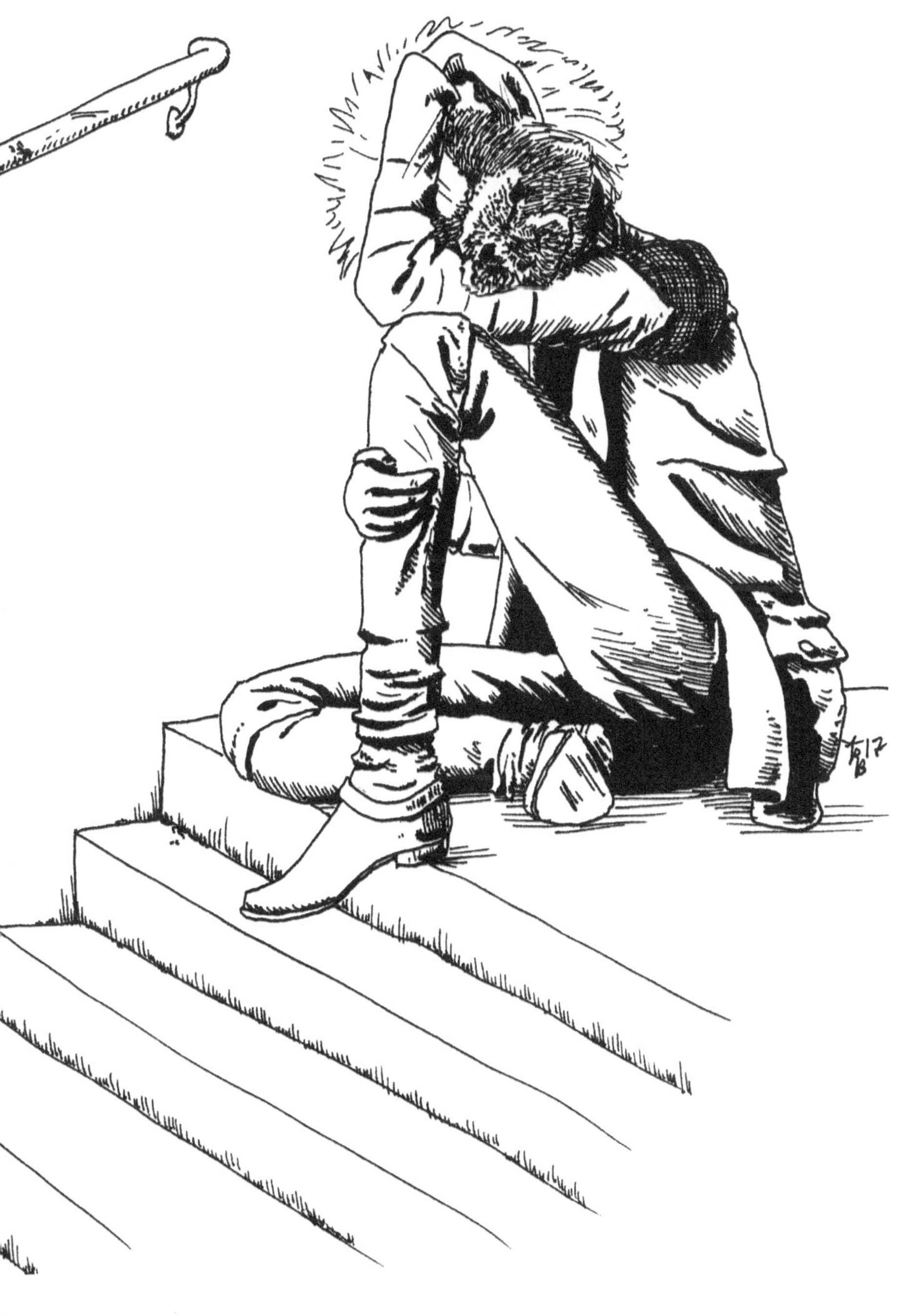

Hailey loves to go camping. But on one trip, she found herself covered with some sort of biolimunescent algae. She removed her contaminated shirt, but it had already soaked through to her skin. The last anyone heard, the CDC was looking for her on the Appalachian Trail where she had taken to hiding.

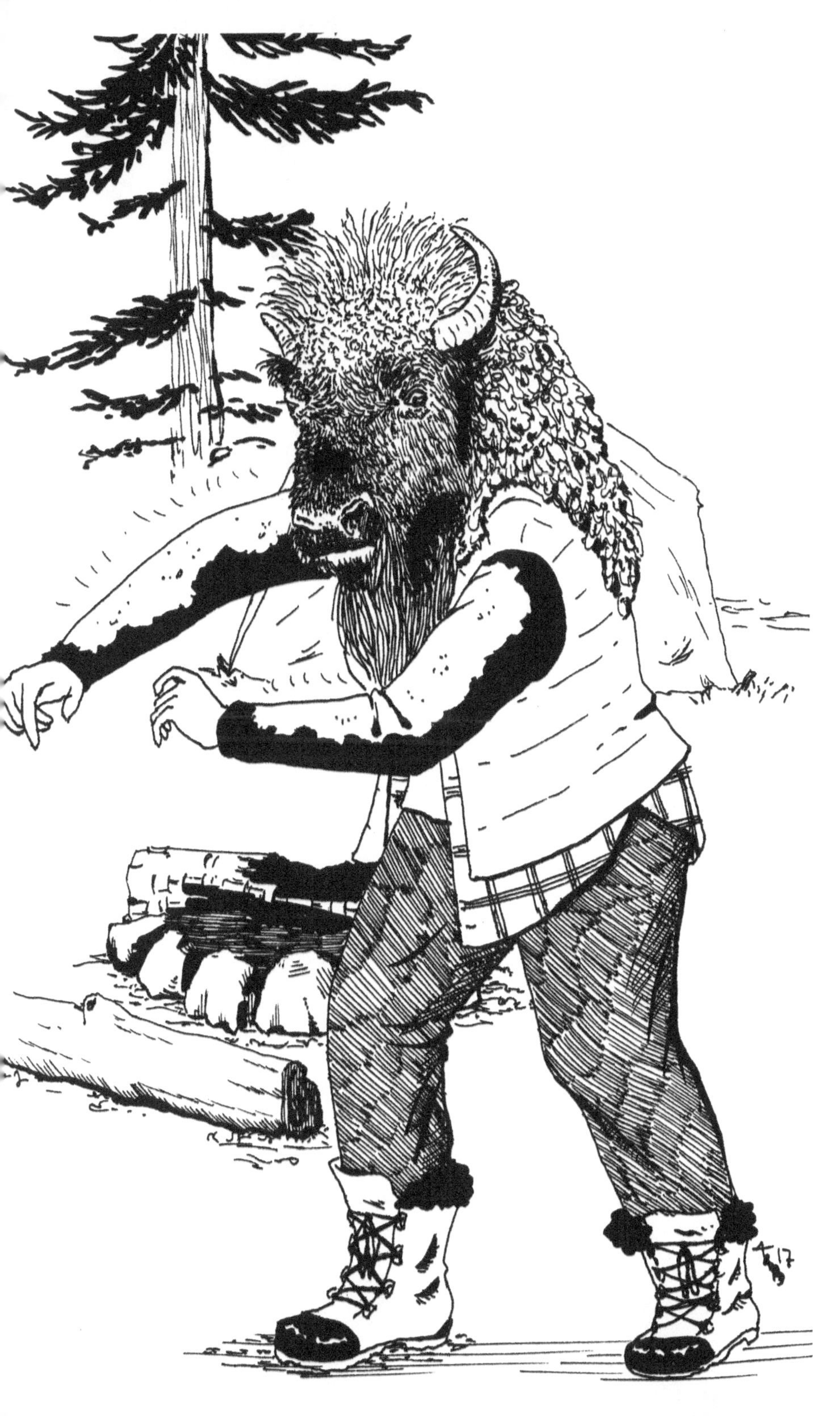

Tamryn is a punk. She loves buckles more than anything else. She finds buckles soothing, as though she is strapping into her own skin. She is less lost in the world now that she wears buckles. Before this discovery, she would wander the streets aimlessly, lost in thought, lost in the past, lost in the future. The buckles hold her to the present.

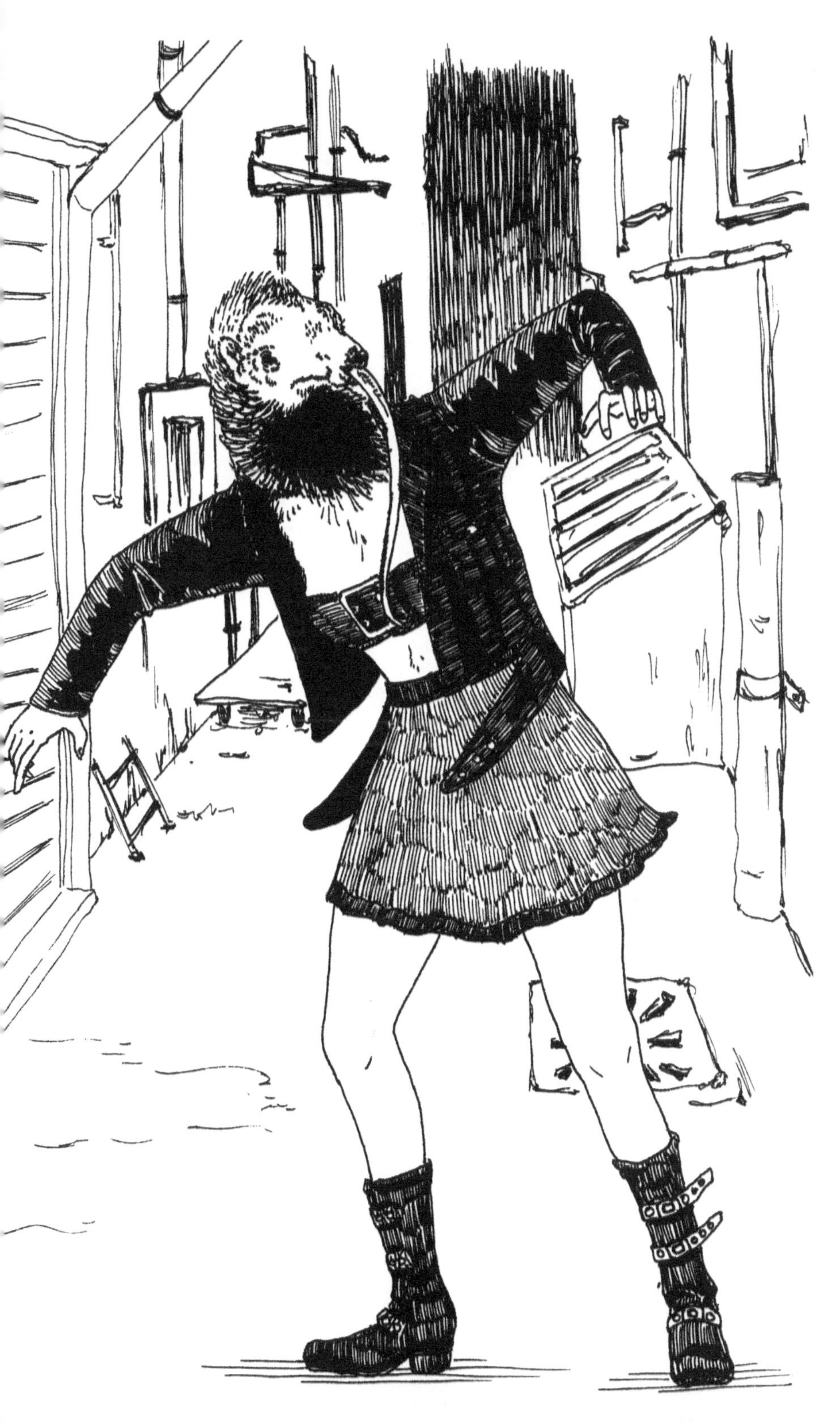

Noëlle is a skeptical lady. She is often found lurking in shadows waiting for things to happen. Unexpected things. She writes them down in her journals. It looks like she always has the same journal, always waiting for the unexpected yet never finding it. But hidden at home is a labyrinth of journals. All looking the same. All full.

Sumatran orangutan, *Pongo abelii*

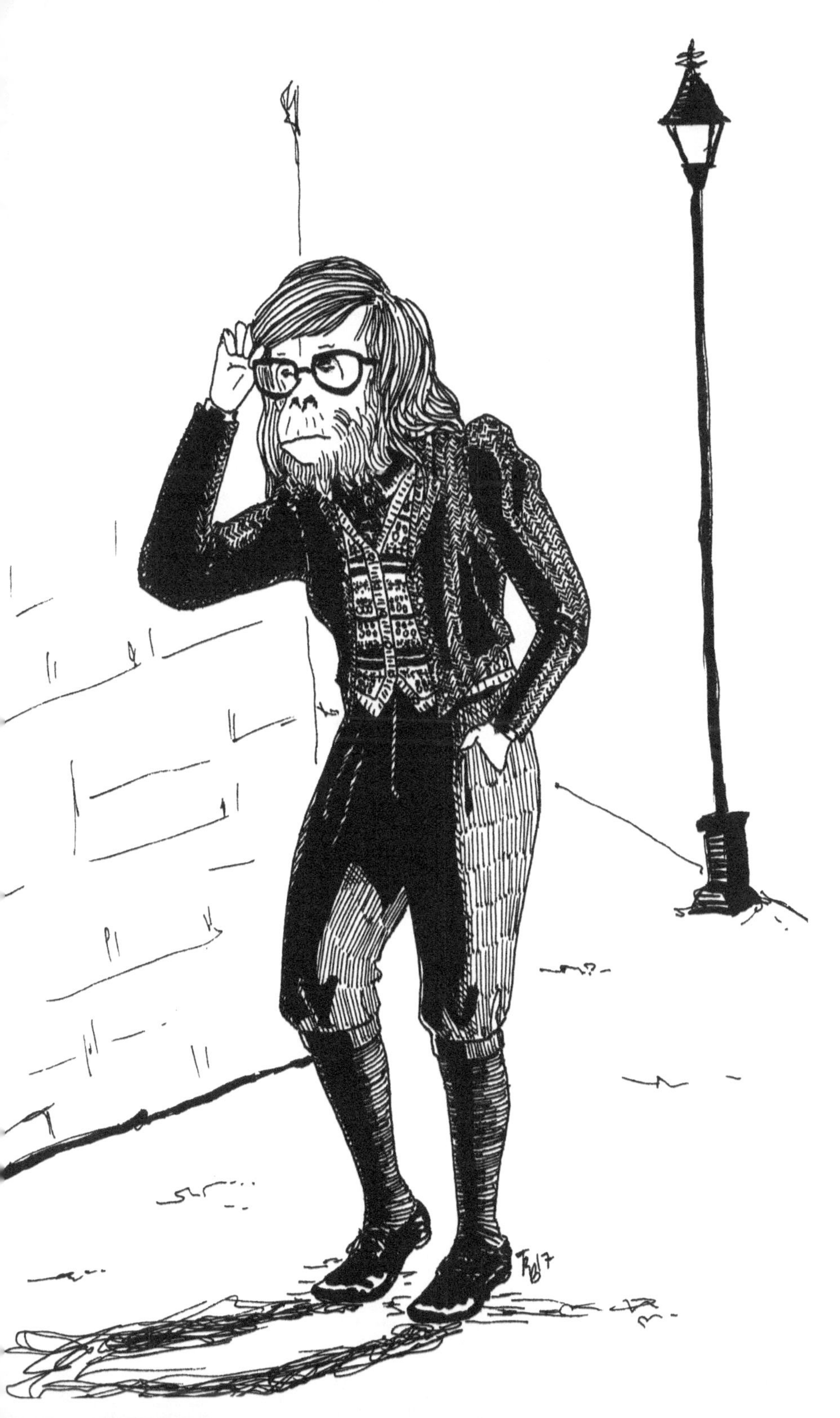

Carla has a penchant for sunbathing. Part of the fun for her is people watching. The sea air lowers their inhibitions. And Carla watches. She watches for mistakes, waits to see their masks fail, the masks they wear in public. She waits to see what they are like inside.

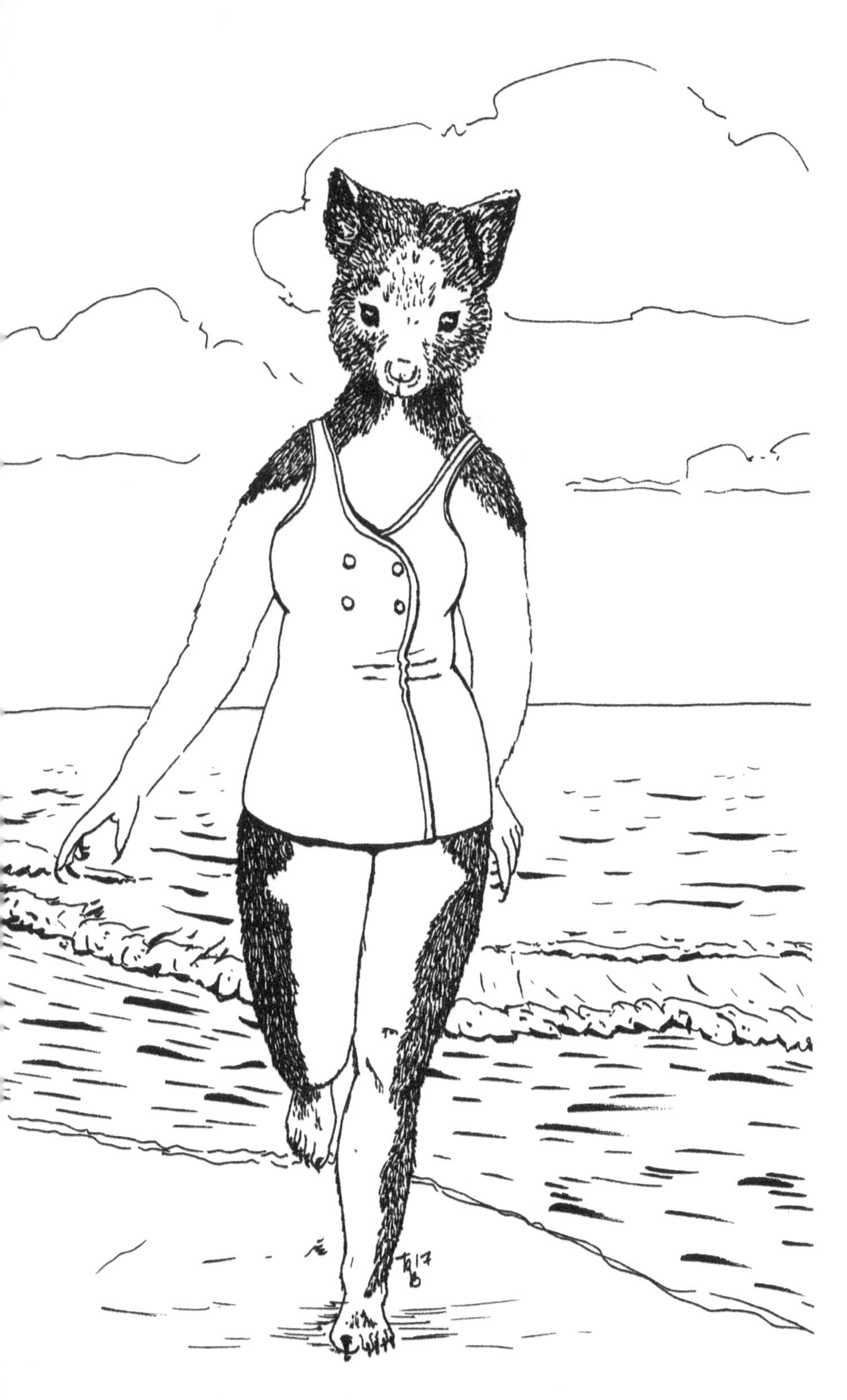

raelyn is a yogi. Through mindful yogic practices, she hopes to attain nirvana. She knows the world and knows its evil. She hopes nirvana will allow her to leave it all behind.

giant panda, *Ailuropoda melanoleuca*

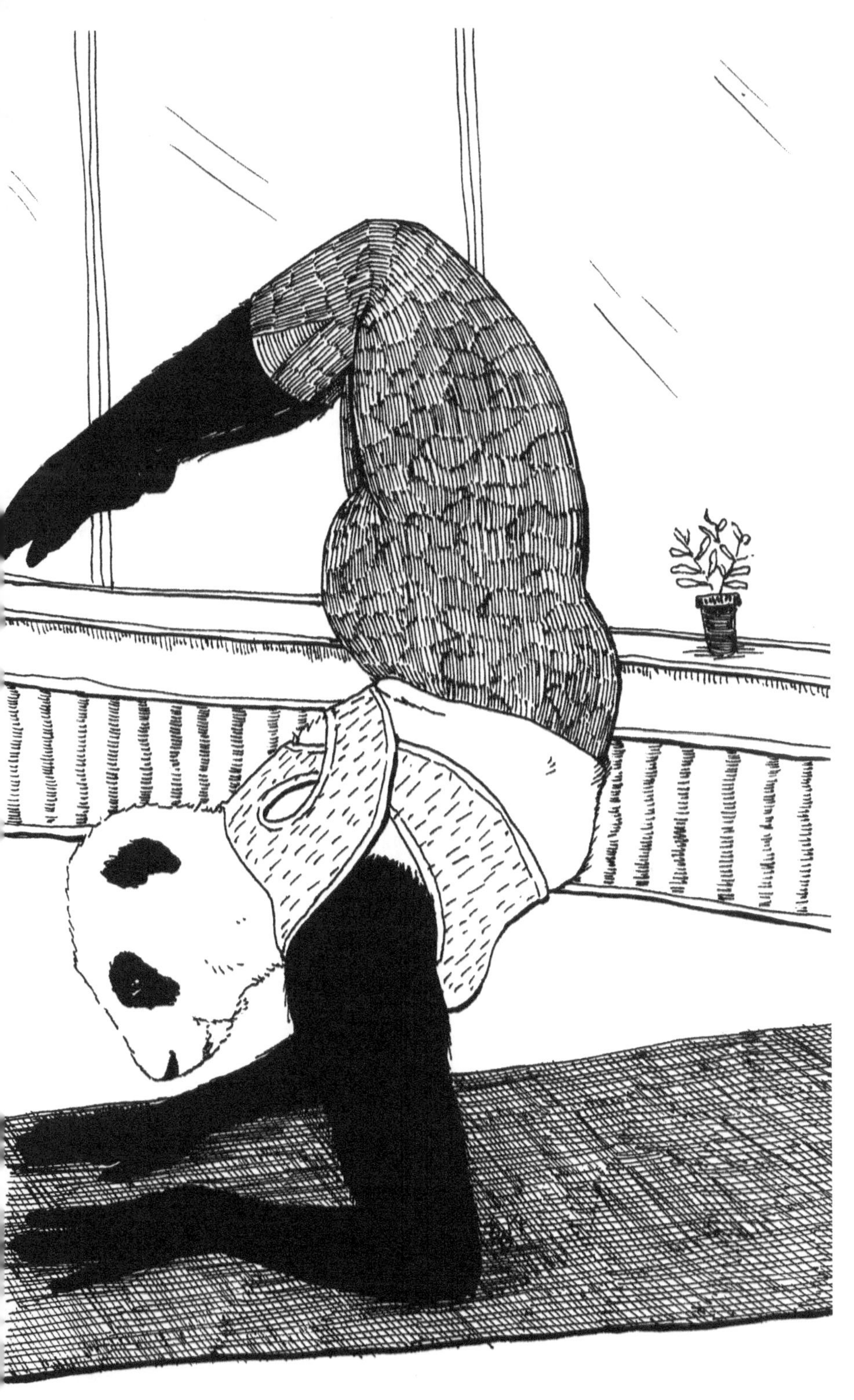

*L*orena is a lady who keeps her eyes on the dirty jobs. She likes to work, and she likes to do the hard work. The tasks no one else wants to do. She started as a crime-scene cleanup specialist, but after watching Mike Row on *Dirty Jobs* she started working in sewers. She became the first US-certified sewer inspector.

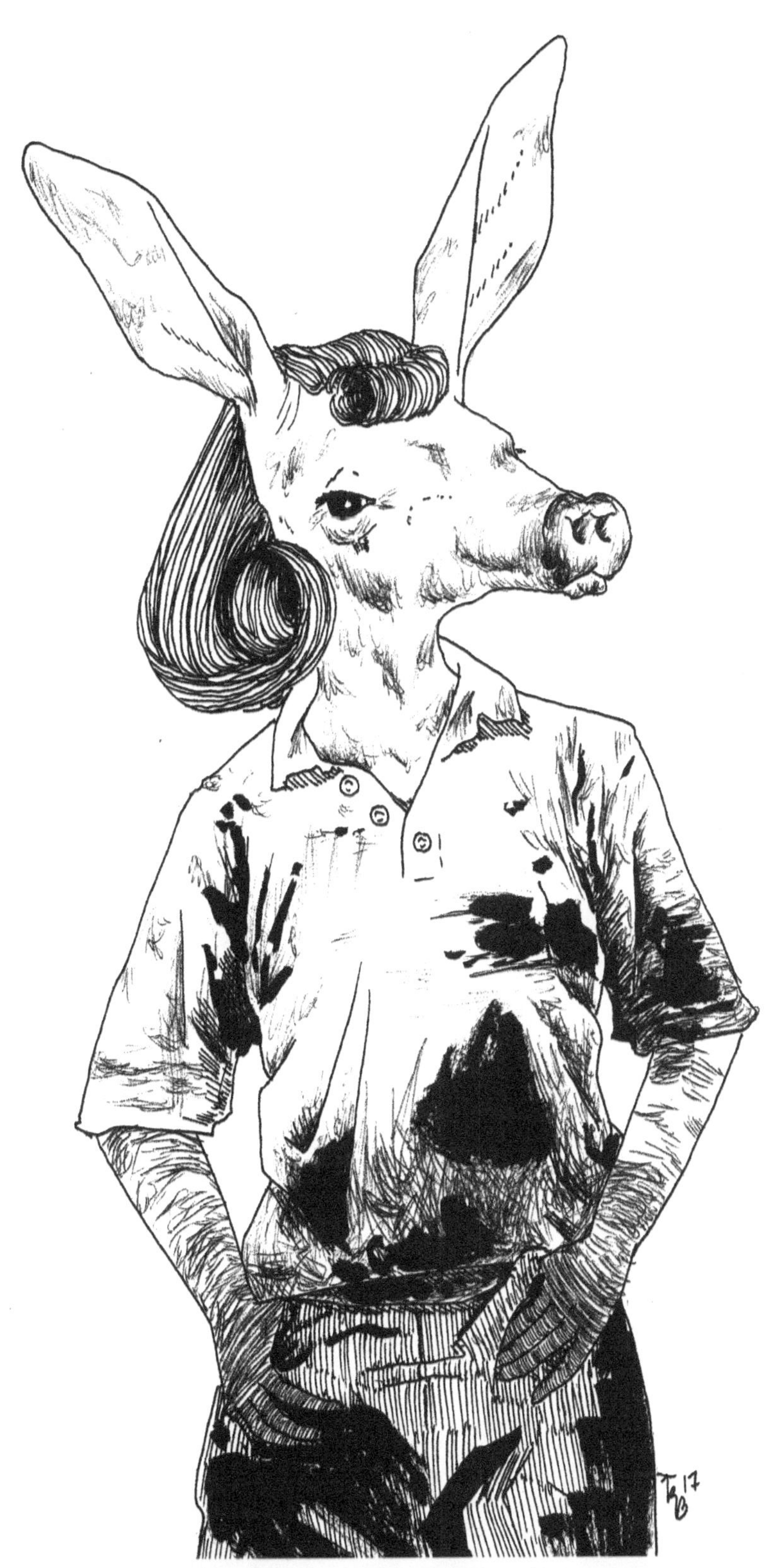

*P*atience is an easily frightened woman. This has left her a rather lonely lot in life because, as opossums do, when she is scared, she releases the stench of death. Even the soft bang of a book on a table will set her off, which is how she lost her job at the library.

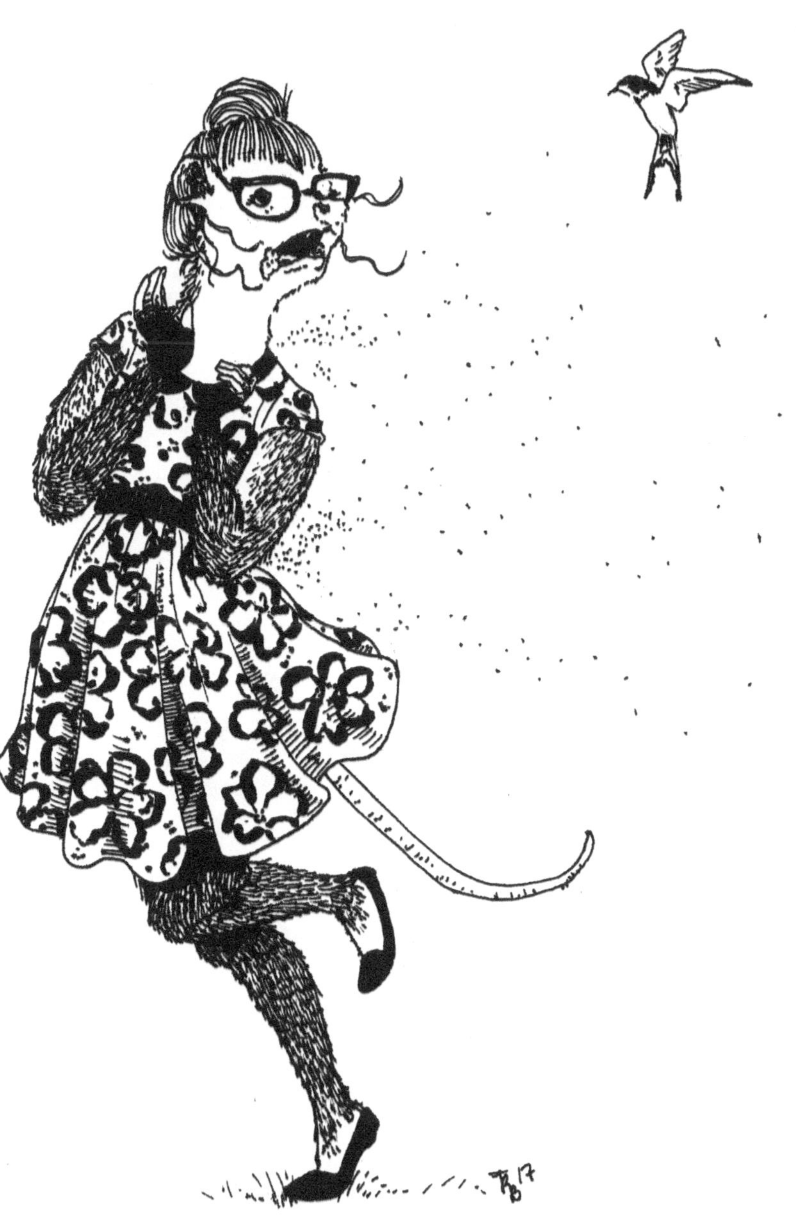

Naïma is a woman with an under-developed left arm. She also lost her lower left leg to a shark. But she has always been a tough and thoughtful young woman and spends most of her time in her study, just thinking. She hasn't told anyone what about. Yet.

domestic yak, *Bos grunniens*

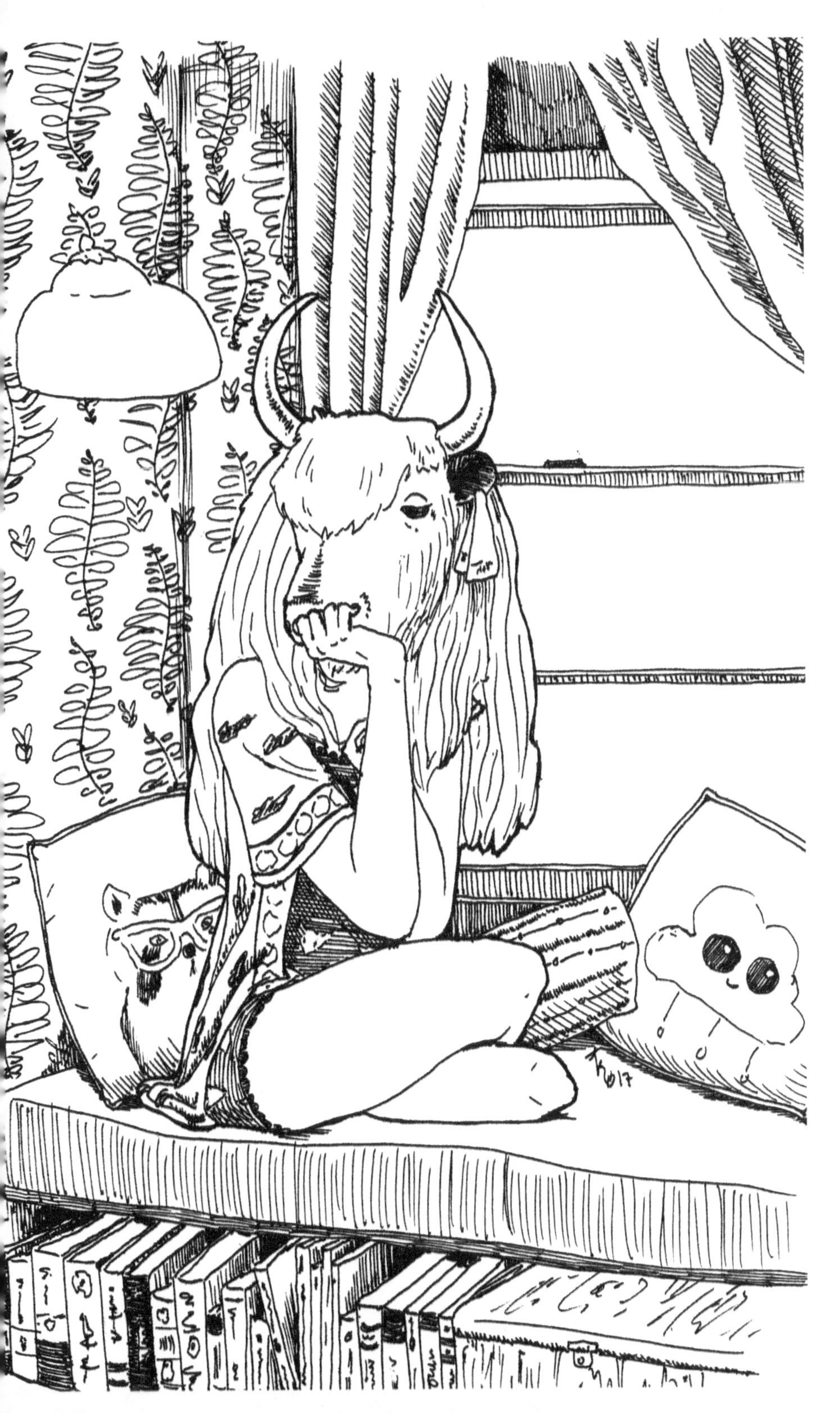

$\mathcal{L}$acey is a lady on a rampage. She lives in a wonderful house sitting back on a large plot of land. The idyllic setting is the perfect place for peace and quite. And loneliness. And forgetting how to interact with other people. At least in a way that leaves them alive. Here she has just remembered that most people cater to social niceties.

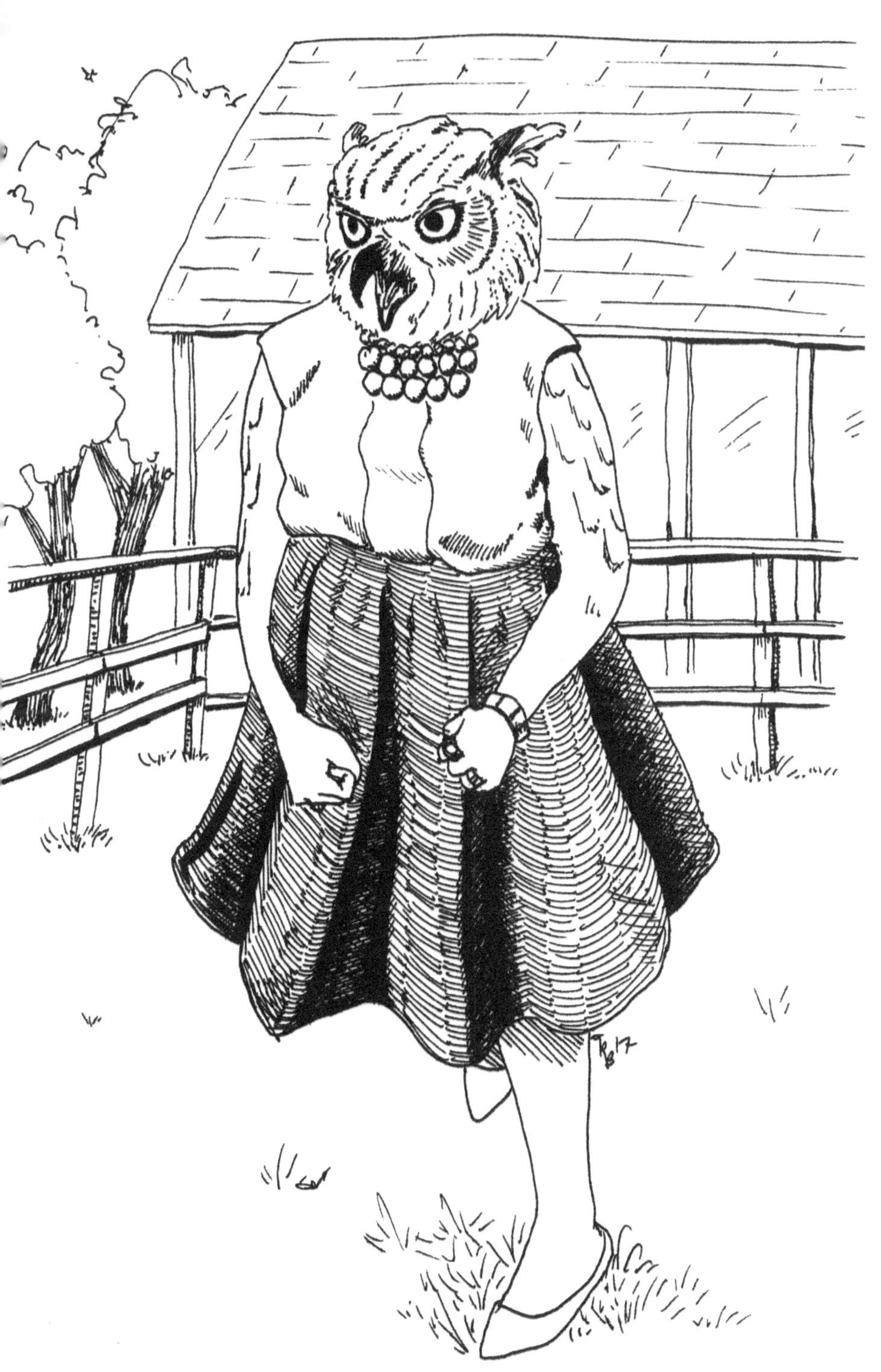

Regina spends a lot of time outdoors. Every weekend, she heads out to a new trail. If she can't find a new trail, she blazes one. Here she is returning from one of the rare trails that she visits repeatedly.

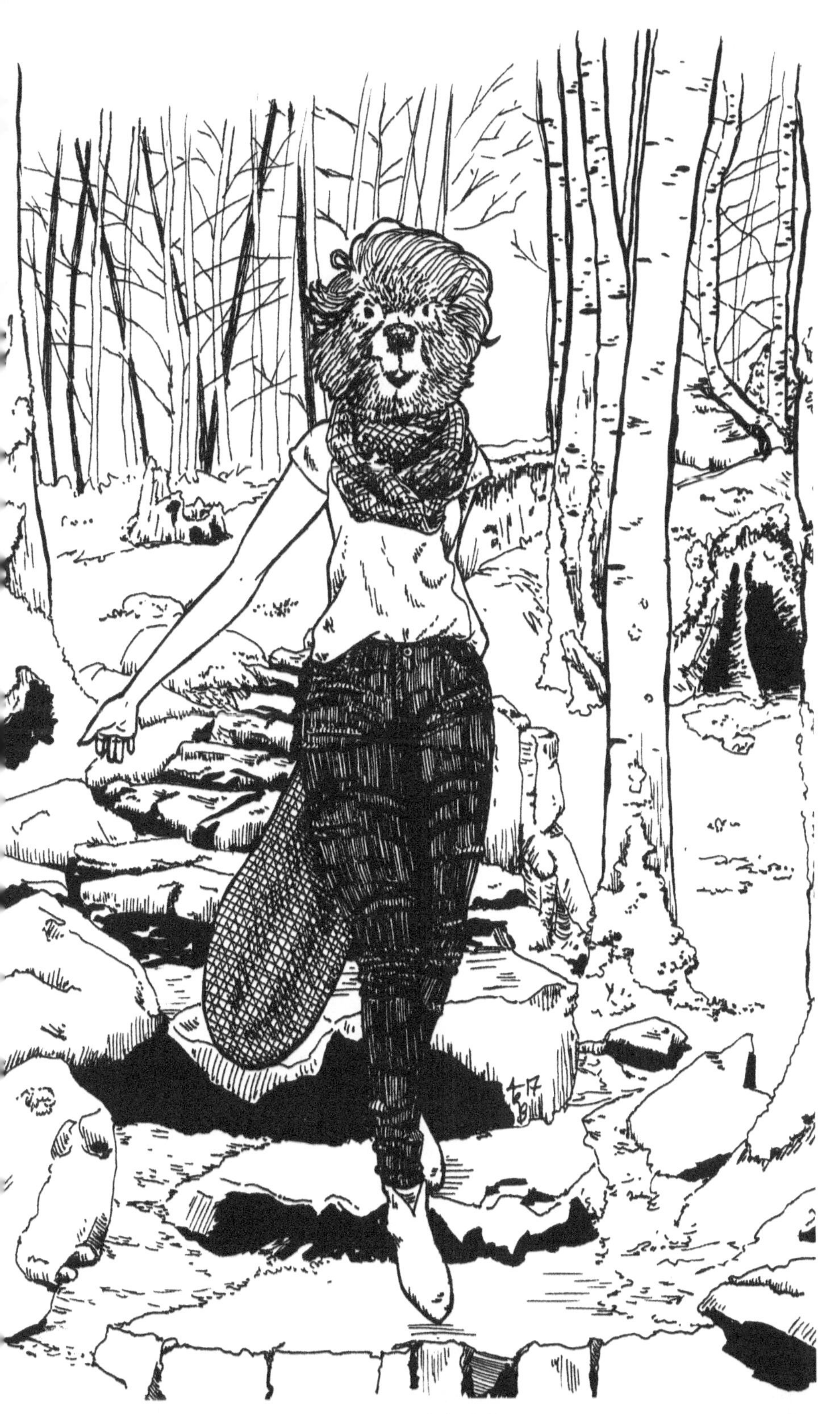

alerie is a runner. Any given day, at any given time, she is
likely to be out running. She runs so far and so often that no
one can talk to her long enough to find out why she is running. But
she is running from something.

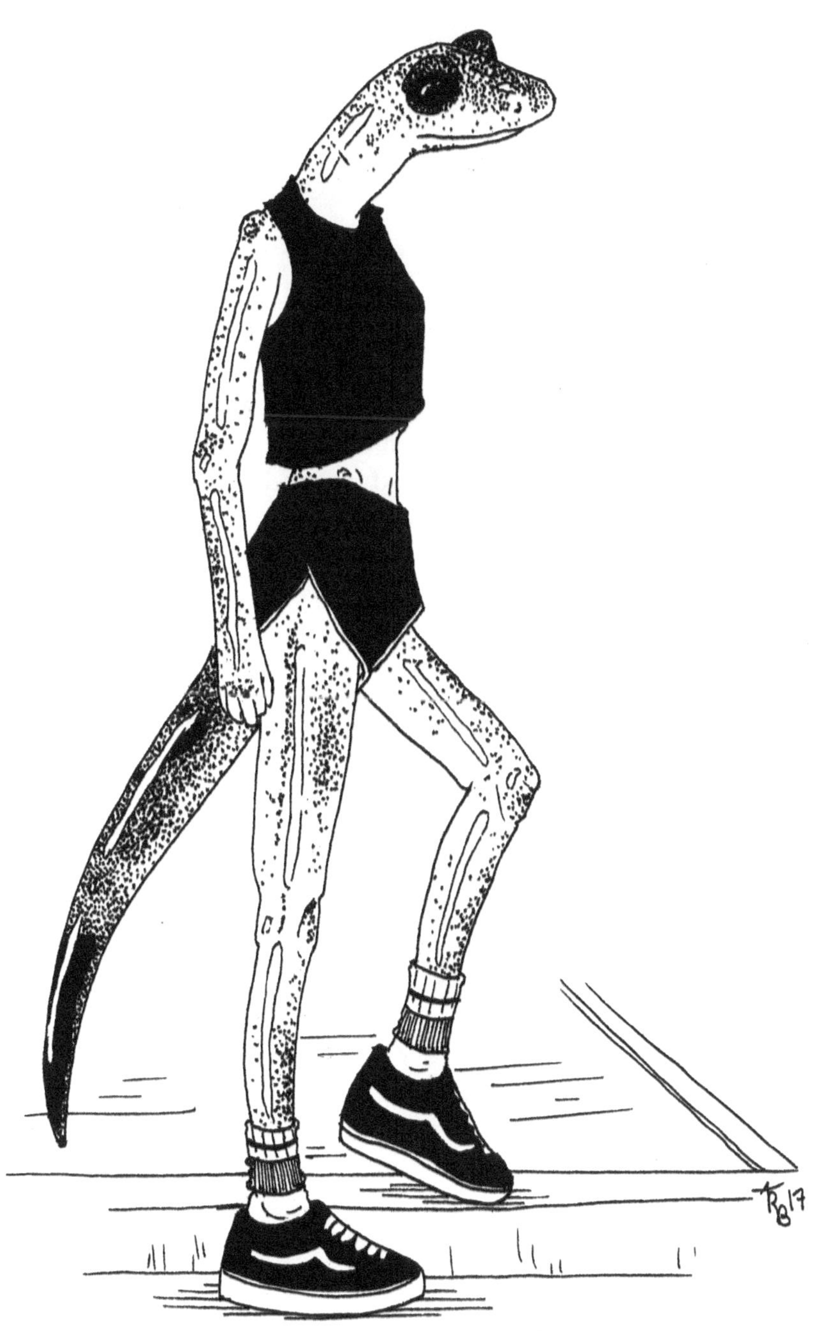

Addisyn might be unable to see, but she can sure smell her tea. Her favorite pasttime is to read in a cafe with a cup of tea. But not for the reading—for the people smelling. The drink smelling. She likes how the different scents waft around the room. Telling her their own little tales.

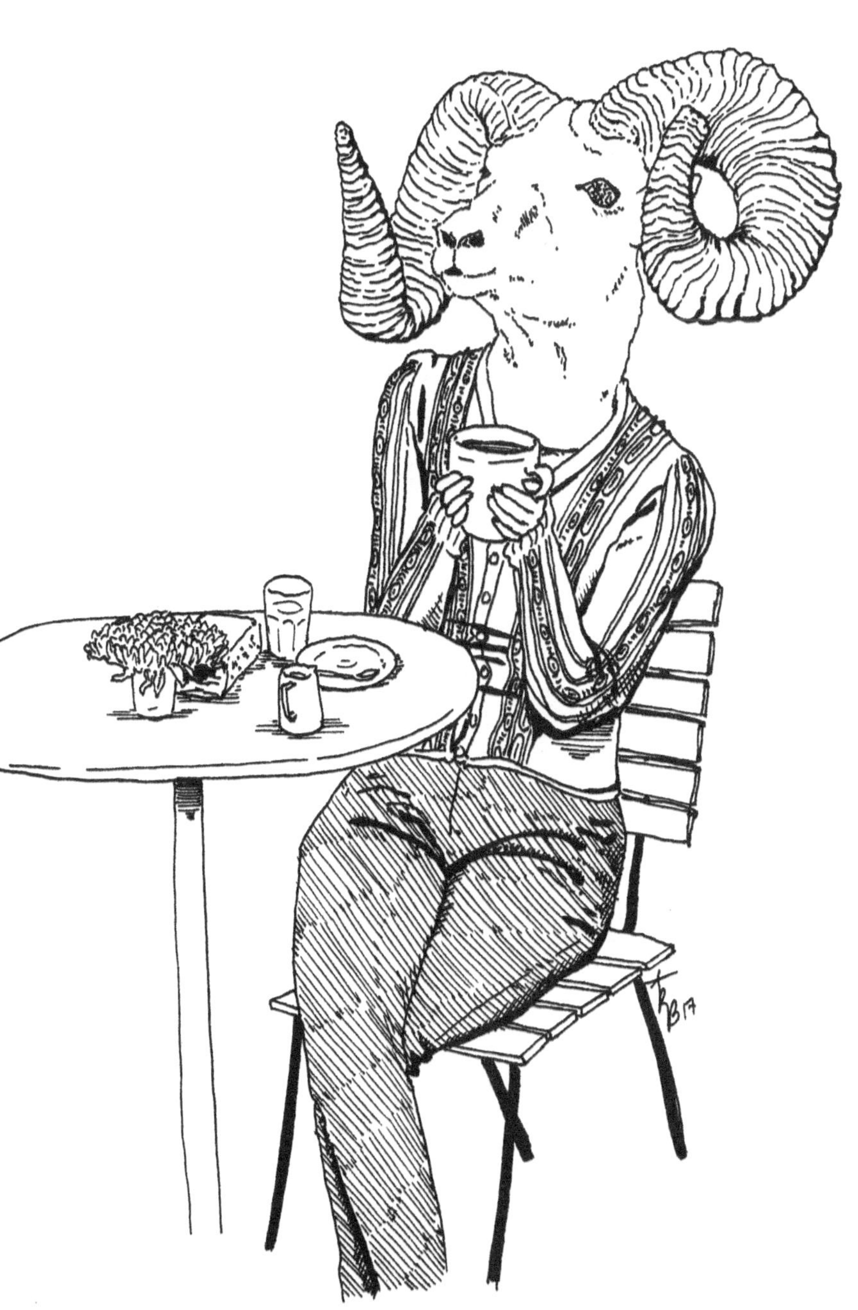

Saige is captain of her own ship and mightily so. She is known far and wide as The Red Saige for her ruthless treatment of prisoners. Her ship, Scourge of the Salt, is stained red with the blood of her victims. The Scourge holds a small crew but for their ferocity, it might as well be a hundred. Saige is the reason people give for not travelling the seas.

scarlet macaw, *Ara macao*

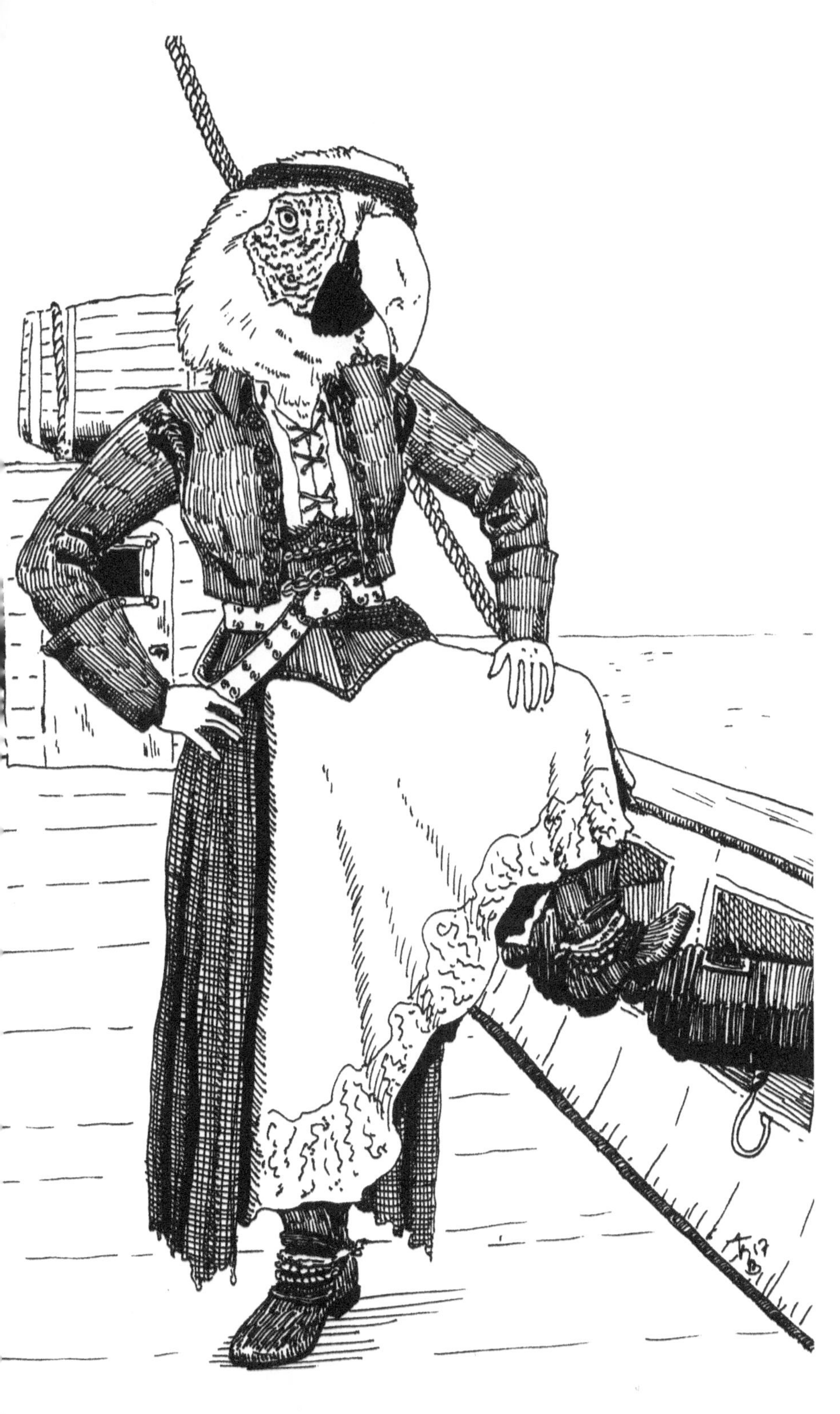

*T*ilia has escaped. Unknowing of her origins, she only remembers the quaint town she awoke in. The empty town. Except . . . she hears noises. Shuffling. Try as she might, she hasn't found any of the culprits. But that might be because she is too scared of what success would show her.

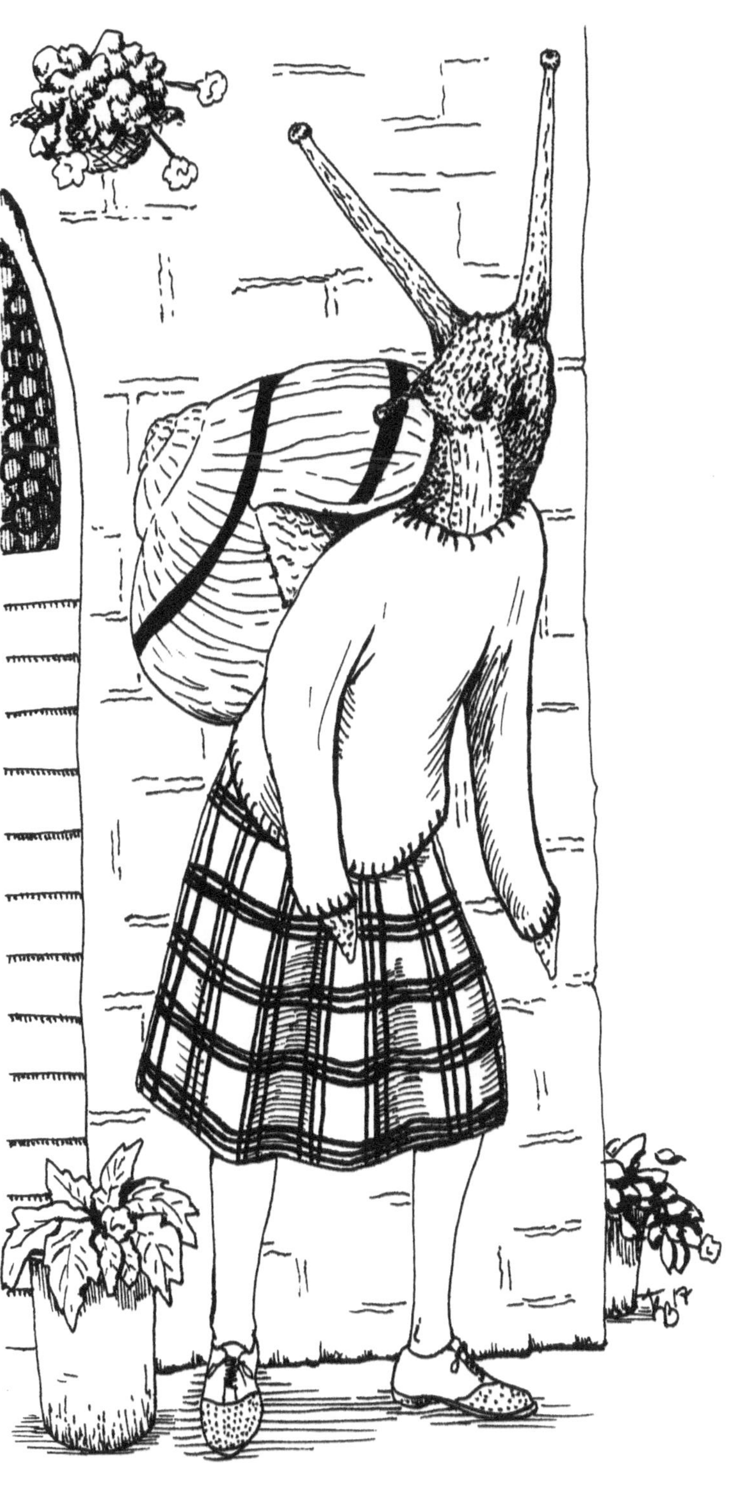

Selena has a steady job, good health insurance, and kind friends.
Yet she is still happy only when she is in a tree, reading a book.

Atlantic puffin, *Fratercula arctica*

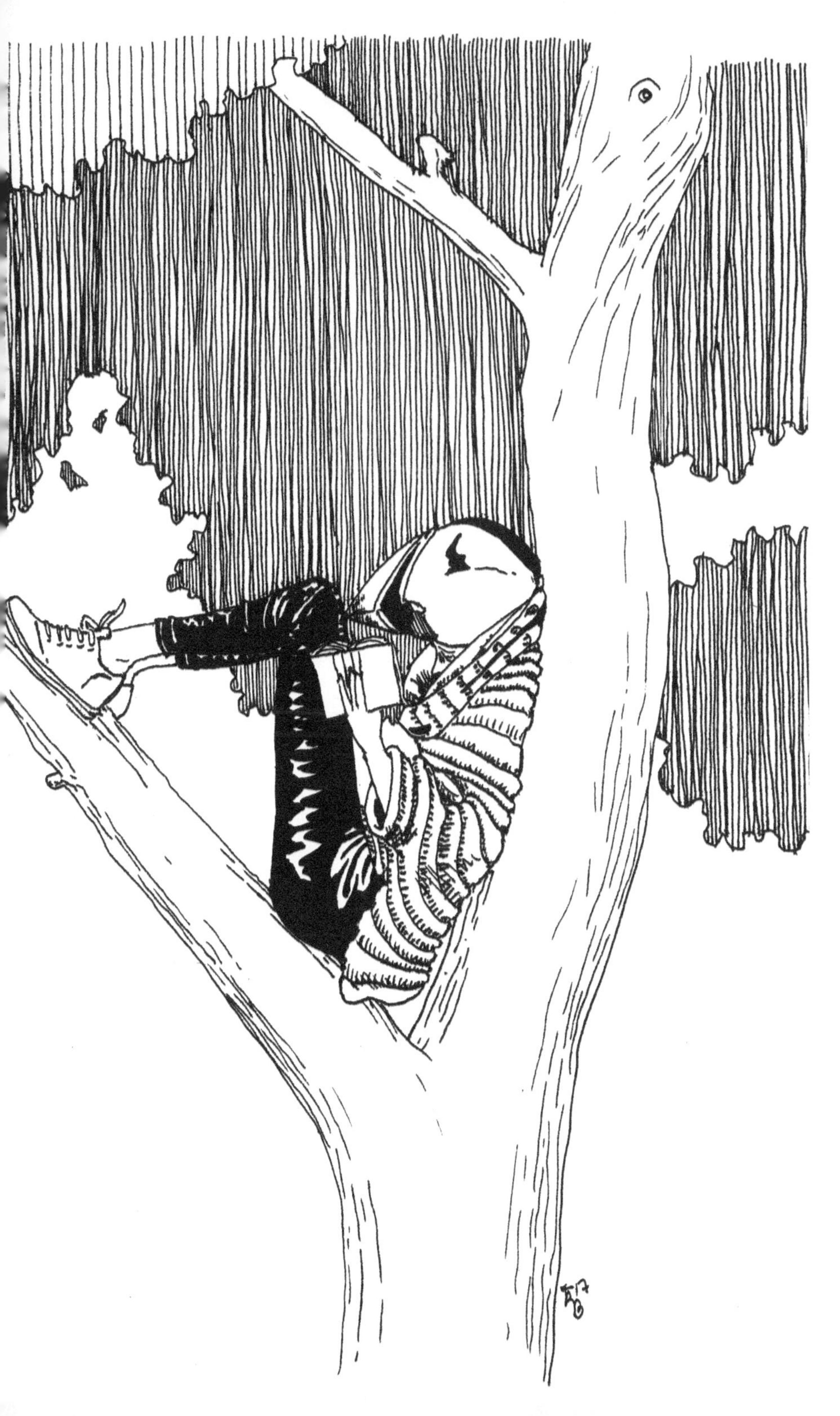

exie loves shoes. She also loves going for long walks in the
woods. These two passions are not always compatible. She has
twisted an ankle more than once on her strolls. On this particular
hike, she is going to sprain both ankles. Hopefully someone will
find her as she crawls on hands and knees, trying to make it back to
her car.

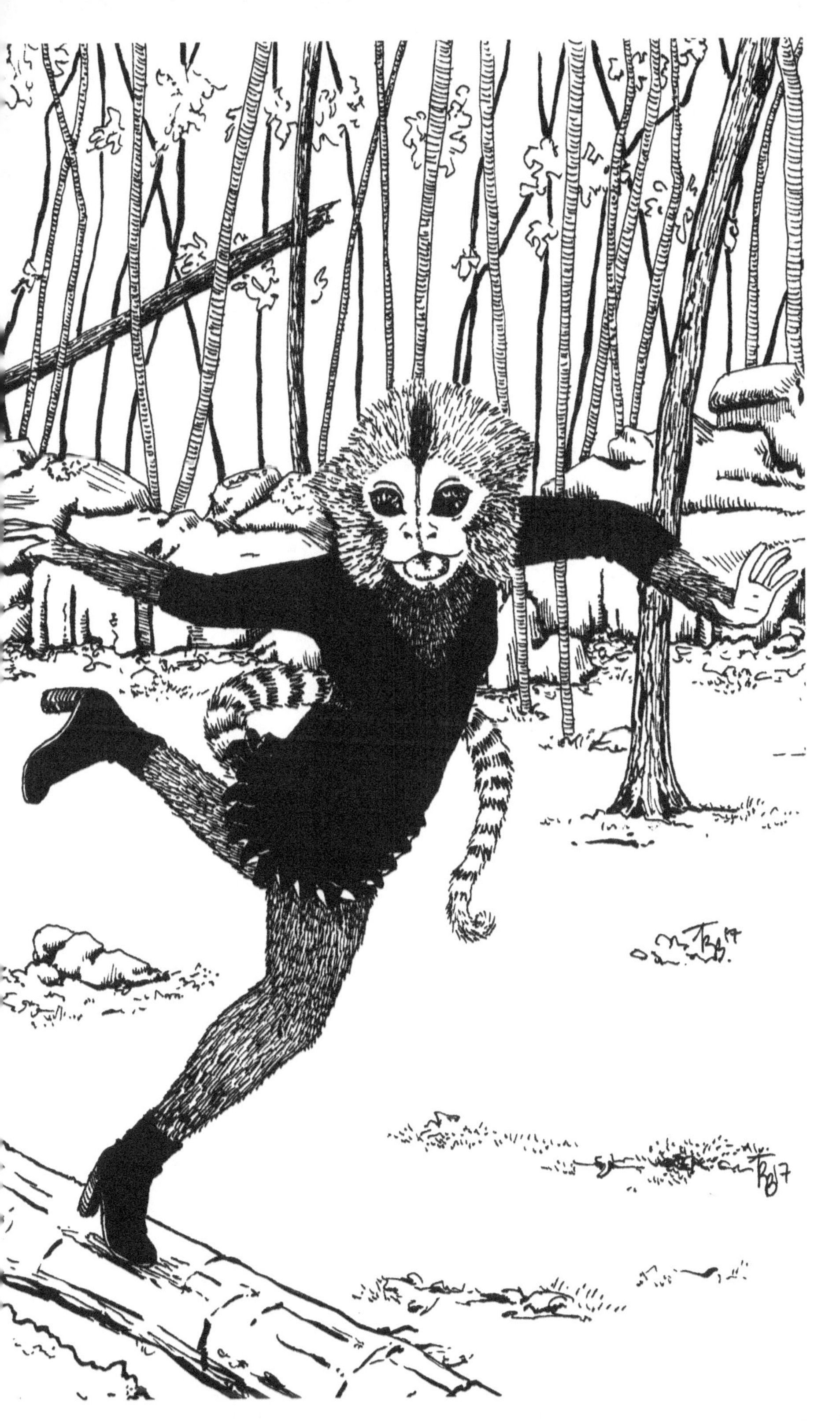

Sophia and Dixie haven't seen each other in 20 years. The courts have finally allowed them to meet again. Everyone expected a tear-filled reunion, but they both think the other is the reason they were caught. They never found out about the lone survivor.

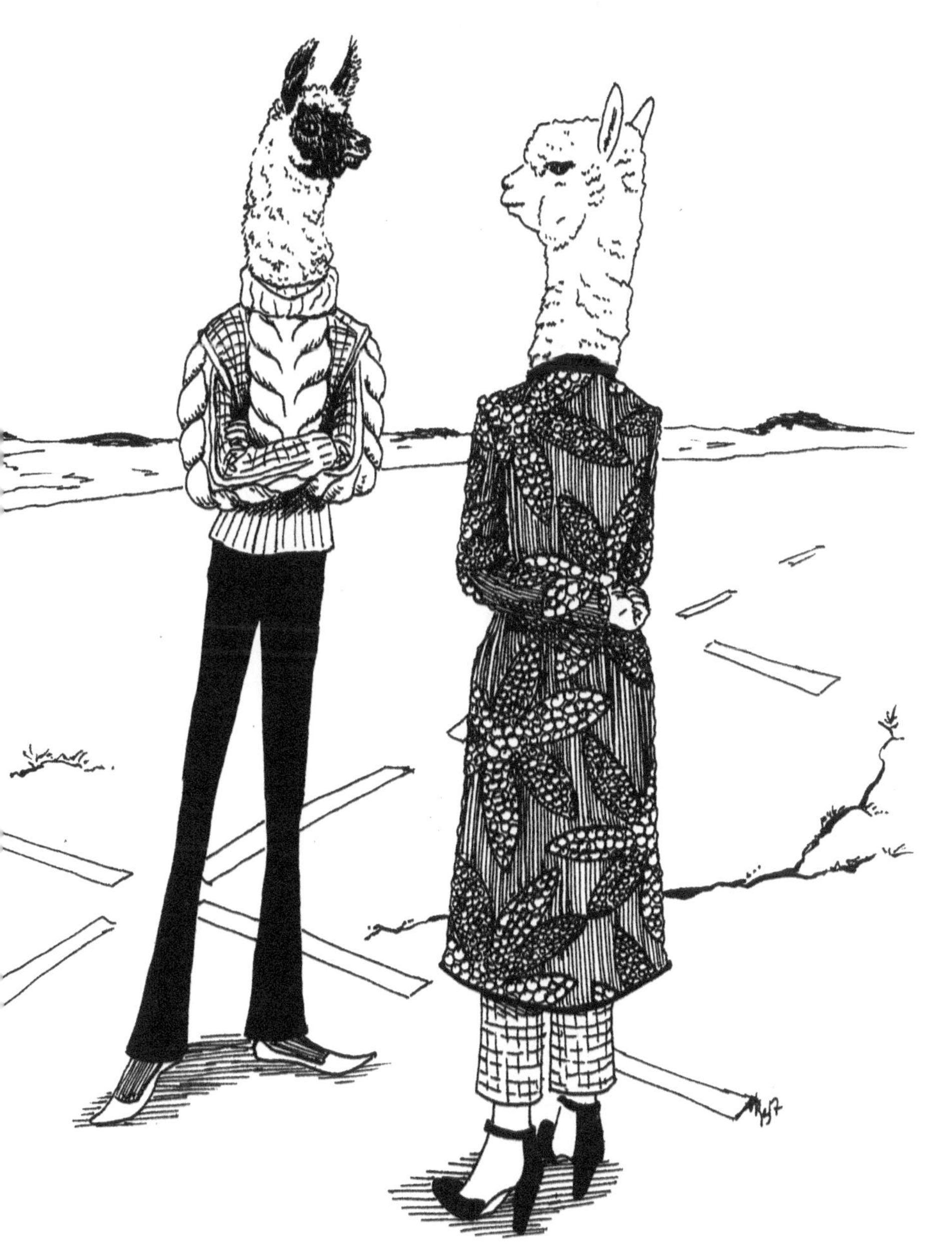

Paola was out for a walk on a country lane when she found a lone glove. She has always found lone items of a pair to be particularly sad. After loosing her own partner, she empathized with them too much. She would often take the lone soul home and make it a new partner—knitting, sewing, or crocheting a near match because a new partner could never hold up to the perfection of the original.

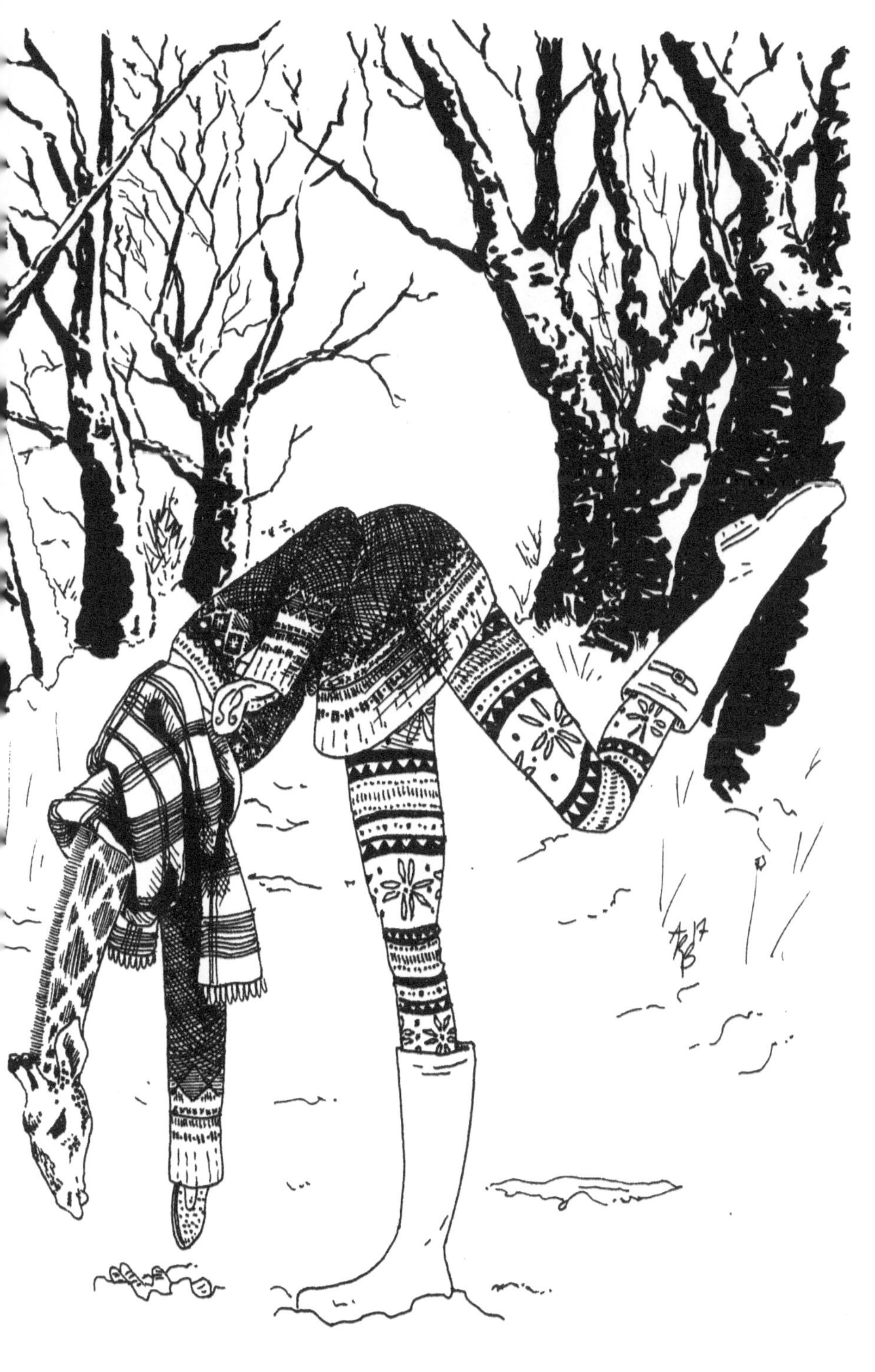

Teia enjoys a good costume party. She was invited to a masquerade ball, but when the party went awry, she hid in the drapery. She waited for the screaming to stop before coming out again.

pink fairy armadillo, *Chlamyphorus truncatus*

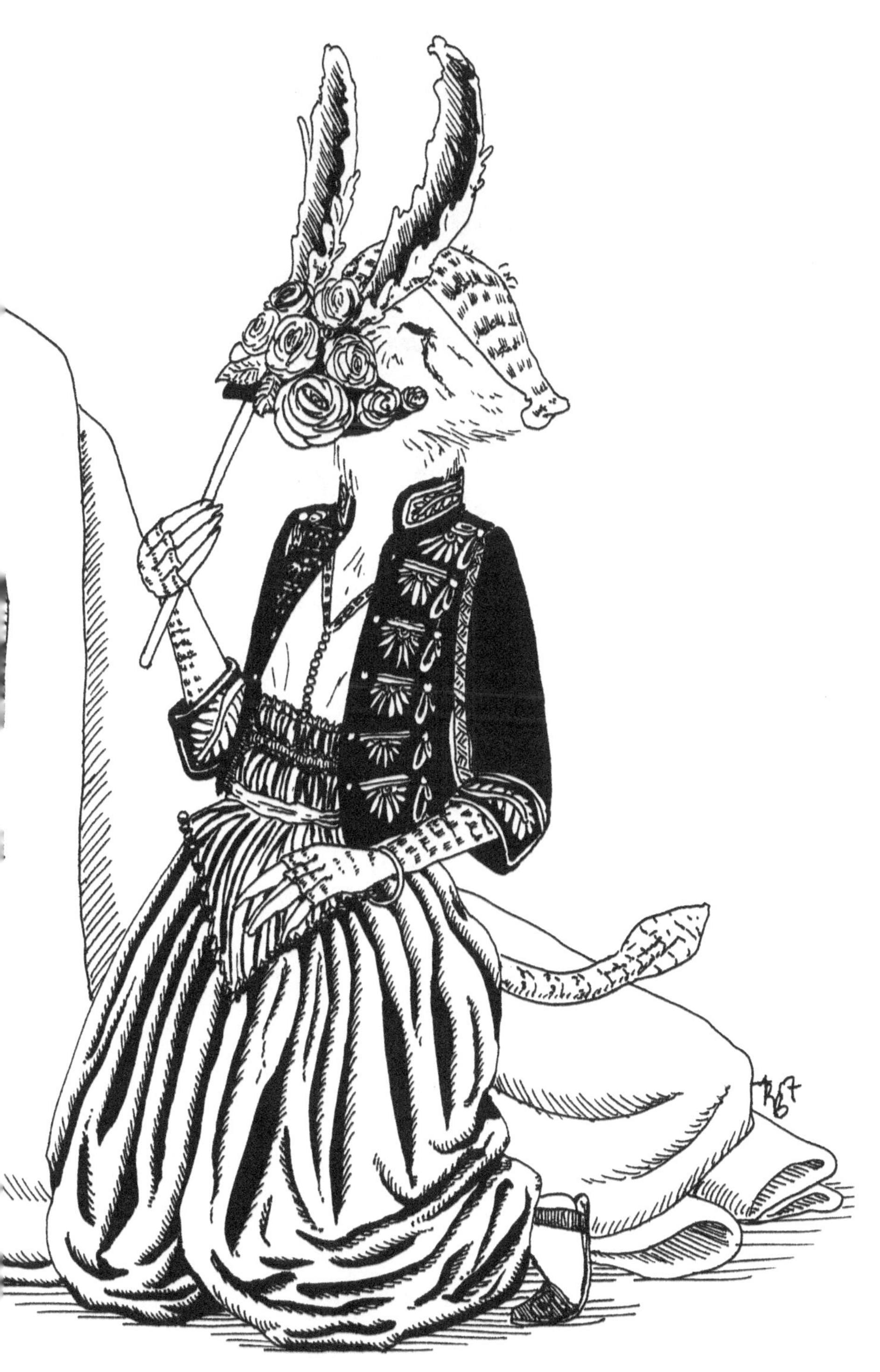

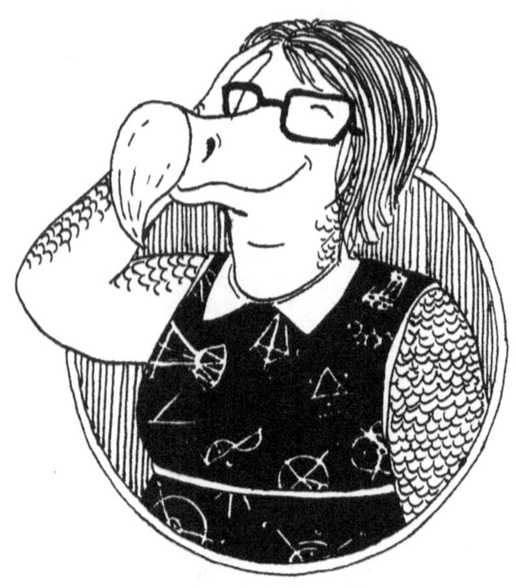

About the Author

Angela Boyle used to live with two corgis, Ernie and Nisa. They spent many great days together. Ernie often modeled Angela's knitting and comics. But now he can't. And they don't. And she doesn't.

Art Portfolio: angelaboyle.flyingdodostudio.com
Editing and Design: publications.flyingdodostudio.com

Twitter, Instagram, Tumblr
angelabcomics

dodo, *Raphus cucullatus*